CW00410094

May your road in life be
free of pot-holes.

Roy Noble.

Roy Noble's Wales

Western Mail Books

Published by Western Mail Books

Editor

John Cosslett

Design and Typesetting

Andrew Jones, Karen Avery, Prakash Parmar.

Prestige Guides, Western Mail & Echo Ltd

Picture Editor

Tim Dickeson

Photographers

Martin Cavaney, James Davies, Martin Ellard, Nigel Hill,
Ian Homer, David Hurst, Brian Jarrett, Rob Norman,
Tony Paradice, Arvid Parry-Jones, Steve Peake,
Tegwyn Roberts, Richard Stanton, Nick Treharne,
Trevor Waters, Iolo Williams

Picture Researcher

Saffron Jenkins

Photo-imaging

Peter Mayled, David Adams, Ross Cummings, Mike Gibbon,
Rachel Grose, Anthony James

Western Mail & Echo Ltd

Printed and bound by

WBC Book Manufacturers Ltd, Bridgend.

Distribution

University of Wales Press.

© Western Mail Books, 1999

All rights reserved. No part of this publication may be reproduced,
stored in a retrieval system, or transmitted in any
form or by any means, electronic, mechanical or otherwise,
without the prior permission of the copyright holder.

ISBN: 1-900477-05-X

$\mathscr{I}$f Wales was toured by the Welsh, each one of us in turn would probably set off on a different compass bearing armed with a map marked Personal Route, or My Wales.

Everyone would have a different portfolio of photographs at the end of the journey, but I dare say there would be some common ground.

There are, after all, so many places with a magnetic drawing power – be they mountain views, seascapes, castles, rolling countryside, centres of myth and legend or conurbations. They all play a part in providing vital historic patches for the quilt that is Wales

This quilt – or carthen if you like – has been well documented in books, tourist material and special-interest publications. I could have included most of those places we know so well again, but I chose not to on this journey. I decided on self-indulgence, and followed a personal "Noble Trail".

I hope you enjoy the tour as much as I did in recalling the places, the people, the views and the variety of experiences that left their marks on my memory.

There is a reason behind each choice, and I confess that, on occasion, the reason may be deeply felt, containing a touch of nostalgic sadness, but in most cases I hope I concentrate on memories that bring a smile to the face, a lightness of the spirit and maybe even a chuckle, as the pages are turned. Perhaps they will remind you of your special places.

If you were given the chance, where in Wales would your journey take you, and why? For what reason would you wish to have that special return ticket to a place you hold dear?

There are still places in Wales of special meaning to me which I have not included for reasons of space, but who knows, perhaps my return ticket this time could become a season ticket, and I could take those other turnings on next year's personal pilgrimage.

Roy Noble

dedicate this book to my wife, Elaine, without whose
support I would not function. She has read and re-read these
scripts and has always indulged my every
whim as, in
life, my
interests and
energies have ebbed and flowed.
She is extraordinary, and it must have been a foggy night for
her when she met me.

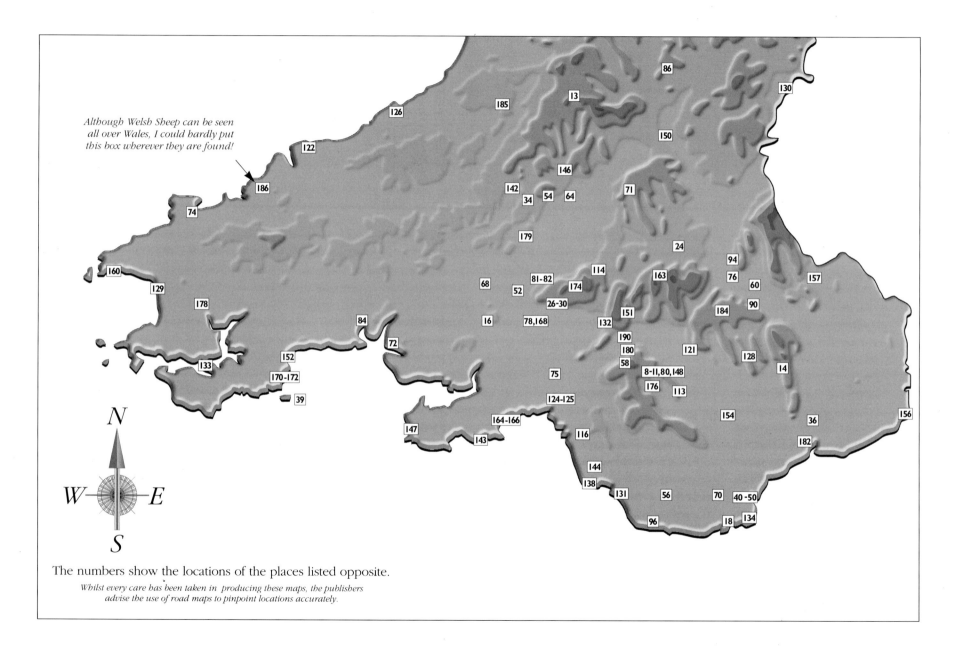

Although Welsh Sheep can be seen all over Wales, I could hardly put this box wherever they are found!

The numbers show the locations of the places listed opposite.

Whilst every care has been taken in producing these maps, the publishers advise the use of road maps to pinpoint locations accurately.

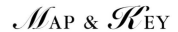

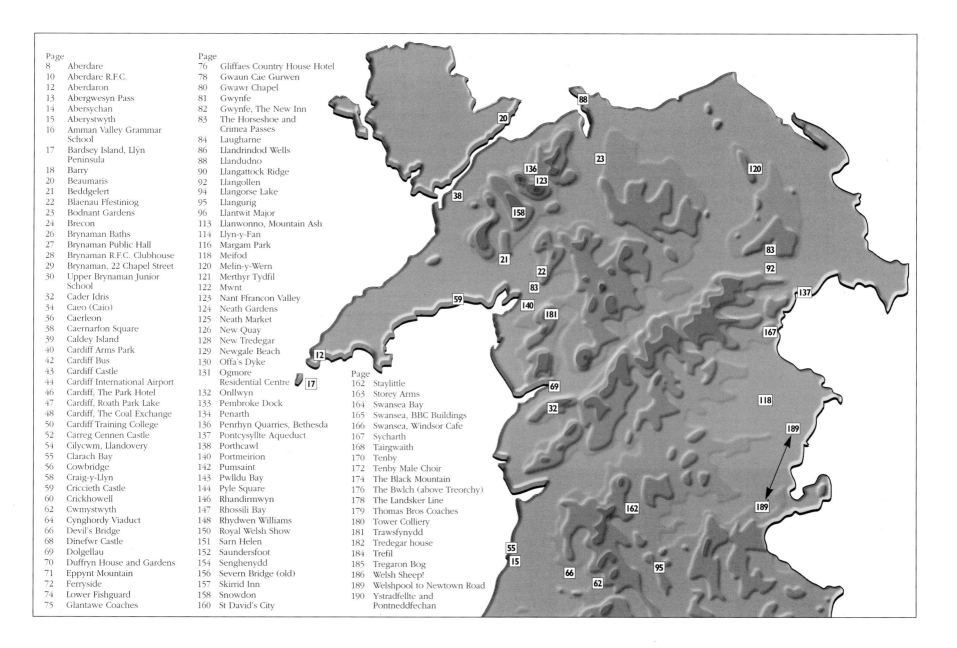

I live in Aberdare because of a woman, my wife Elaine, and although my roots are further west in Brynaman, the Cynon Valley has now become my home. I remember the first occasion I came to the Cynon Valley very, very well. I travelled up from Cardiff on a Red and White bus to meet Elaine's parents for the first time. It was a Sunday and I was due there for lunch. I asked the bus driver to put me out on Aberaman Bridge. I have to say that I was very impressed with the house because they had a bathroom indoors and an automatic washing machine as well. Our bathroom at home in Brynaman hung on a nail outside the back door. It was near the semi-detached toilet we shared with next door. My mother didn't have an automatic washing machine for years, nor did she have a cooker. For some illogical reason I think she thought that all this smacked of cheating in household chores. All her cooking was done in the oven at the side of the fire grate, but she eventually condescended to a washing machine which had a roller attached to it. Aberdare has been good to me and I have enjoyed my life there. Elaine and I have many friends and they certainly keep my feet on the ground. Broadcasting, after all, is just a job, and there can be no airs and graces in this area. I remember in my early days of broadcasting going into a pub in Aberdare and being asked by one of the locals, "Was it you on the radio this morning, Roy?" My chest swelled a little and I answered, "Yes, yes it was." "Wasn't much bloody good, was it?" he said. Thinking about his comments later, I promised myself that if ever ego reared its head, I would try desperately hard to put it at least in my back pocket, or, better still, throw it away completely.

Now here's an interesting tale. Aberdare R.F.C. for many years were called Aberaman R.F.C. Around the turn of the century, they were originally Aberdare R.F.C. but were banned from the Welsh Rugby Union for paying their players. Subsequently, they moved two miles down the valley to Aberaman and continued playing under the new name. You could call them a club ahead of their time, because now most clubs are paying their players. I am a member of the club and I enjoy my visits there. On a Sunday morning there is a group of old stagers who meet in the corner of the lounge bar and put the world to rights. The conversation is not always about rugby. It is about world events, local happenings and scandals. And if the Government could ever tap into the ingenuity and intellectual power here, then along with taxi drivers and barbers, they would have a great think tank that would clear up any international problem in the hour and a half prior to Sunday lunch. The club has a colourful chairman, and during my days as a rugby referee of very menial ability and low standing, he would often call upon my services, even after I had retired, saying that the booked referee had not turned up. I was usually in charge of the 3rd XV, which is always a mixture of young boys who are keen and making their way upwards and the more mature breed who are on their way down and will put the cigarette out on the touch line before they take the field. As the chairman works for a large supermarket supplier, I was usually paid in washing powder. I confess to a super-large box but it was usually given to me upside down as there was a hole in the bottom of it. There is a great camaraderie in the club, and like many other clubs in Wales, it is the true base of Welsh rugby football. It nurtures the game. The club is not, at the time of writing, in the first five divisions of the Welsh Rugby Union leagues, but it runs several sides from 1st XV all the way down to junior-school boys. Most of the upper-crust clubs of Wales, of course, don't bother with that kind of commitment. The game at this level is also played on most occasions with the right priority view of life. I remember standing on the touchline one Saturday when there was a skirmish and a ruck-and-maul nearby. As the opposing hooker bounced to his feet, he noticed me standing there and shouted out, "Excuse me, who is the mystery voice on the programme these mornings in that competition of yours?" You have to admire a man who, in the heat of battle, still has time to wonder about intellectual challenges.

I visited Aberdaron on more than one occasion. It is the launch pad if ever you want to cross to Bardsey Island. To get to it you have to pass down the magnificent Llŷn Peninsula and you do have a feeling of travelling through the ancient western reaches of Wales and of being on the edge of the country. I have spent many nights there and, always, the company has been convivial. In essence, a place is its people, and if you find them friendly and welcoming then the image of the town or village stays clearly in the mind for all the best reasons. Aberdaron, like Abersoch, has much to commend it in terms of scenery and welcome.

Abergwesyn to me is a symbol of wild Wales. George Borrow, in his famous journey through Wales in the last century, had the perfect title to his book *Wild Wales* and this place fits the phrase exactly. Abergwesyn Pass leads north from Llanwrtyd Wells and eventually, if you turn left, towards Tregaron. Just beyond the waters of the Llyn Brianne reservoir you come across a remote but very famous Welsh chapel – Soar-y-Mynydd. Most of the famous preachers of Wales have preached here, and you cannot but be impressed by the remoteness of this place of worship, which is a symbol of Welsh nonconformity.

When I was in college, which had a strong bias towards P.E., I myself was doing geography – more of a thinker than a doer, I suppose. During our course we had to undertake two surveys. One was in the Vale of Glamorgan, the other was in Gwent. A friend of mine named Thomas Gilmor Nimrod Jones, who was from Saron near Ammanford and oddly enough attended the same school as myself – Amman Valley Grammar School – before moving on to college, was to be my companion on this survey. We have quite a unique photograph of ourselves standing on Abersychan Station during one of our survey days. The station is no more, neither is the railway line, but the road north to Blaenavon passes this way. It was on this survey that I also tracked down the hamlet whose name I first noticed in Cardiff bus station – British, which stands on the hill above Abersychan.

I have to include Aberystwyth because it always came third behind Porthcawl and Barry whenever trips were planned from my village. We would either travel to Aberystwyth via Aberaeron or we would take the longer route up to Rhayader and then on through the Elan Valley with all its beautiful reservoirs. I was, initially, disappointed that Aberystwyth did not have a sandy beach, but I always enjoyed my stay and the walk along the promenade to kick the bar at the end before returning again was a must. I also remember playing for Brynaman Rugby Football Club in Aberystwyth. It was always a stay-away fixture in that we stayed away for the night – not overnight but just for the evening up until about 11 o'clock. At about 11.30 on a Saturday evening on these Aberystwyth visits, the team bus was to be seen roaming around the town looking for stray stragglers. On one occasion I was amongst four players "missing" as the bus toured. We had become friendly with a few locals of the opposite gender. The evening held promise in the stars that shone across Cardigan Bay and every time I hear the song Under the Boardwalk, I am reminded of that night, for I hadn't seen Aberystwyth Pier from that angle before. But that is another story for another book.

I attended this school from 1954 to 1961. There are many tales to tell but I will concentrate on one. During our "maturing" years those of us courting with girls from the school had certain Friday night arrangements.

In winter months, when the weather was cold, we needed some ingenuity of thought to provide shelter for our developing relationships on Saturday nights. Consequently, if, as was usual, the dates were arranged for Saturday, locks were released on the school cloakroom windows on Friday afternoon. Then, when frosty Saturday evenings threatened, we all sneaked to the school and quietly entered the cloakrooms – just for a bit of warmth, you understand. Sometimes, after a cinema visit first, you had to head through the darkness quite quickly just to get some reasonable space in a very crowded cloakroom.

I had the good fortune to visit Bardsey Island during filming some years ago. The journey across from Aberdaron can be difficult, especially if the currents that swirl through Bardsey Sound are playing up. The island was wild, lonely and very atmospheric and there were two couples living on it when we visited. One elderly couple ran the only farm on the island and they were very hospitable indeed. Another couple had a joint purpose to their stay. One was an artist, and her partner was the wildlife warden. They took their supplies from Aberdaron on the mainland and occasionally they were caught at Aberdaron if a storm blew up preventing their return. A rumour suggested that they sometimes checked with weather forecasters and, if storms were due, they deliberately set off for the mainland, hoping to be "trapped" in some welcoming hostelry. I cannot believe that to be true; men are not like that.

Village trips to me as a youngster meant one of three places –
Porthcawl, Aberystwyth or Barry. On the South Wales coast, Barry
had the edge over Porthcawl because it was further.

The buses or coaches would park in what seemed to me to be a
line of garages around the headland of Nell's Point, where Billy
Butlin built his holiday camp. The great shelters on the
promenade along the beach at Whitmore Bay reminded me of the
Parthenon in Athens. I think it was the columns that did it.

I was intrigued by the line of cafes and seaside shops along the
bottom end of the Barry Island fairground. Particularly those
where you could go and eat your own sandwiches as long as you
bought their tea, but you had to go into the back room to do so,
and sit on long forms at long tables. People who bought their fish
and chips or egg and chips were allowed to sit in the front part of
the cafe.

Barry Island was sand, sea, candyfloss and toffee apples, with an
hour in the fair before we went back on the bus. On the journey
home there was a collection for the driver in a cap and a singsong
all the way. There weren't any hills on the way home, but we
were "coming round the mountain" for mile after mile.

I had the good fortune to visit Beaumaris when I did a series for BBC Television on the Castles of Wales. We decided upon just 10 castles for the first series and each castle was allocated only five minutes of air time. It was enough history to get you interested, I hope, but not quite enough to get you bored. I enjoyed the tour immensely and I remember Beaumaris for the superb vista it provided as I looked south towards Snowdonia. There are few sights to impress as much, I am sure, as Snowdonia, especially on a fine day, when all the peaks are clear, and their shoulders are shadowed by the colours of the day.

The name means the grave of Gelert, the brave dog who defended Prince Llywelyn's child against a wolf and was killed by his master, who mistakenly thought that the blood-spattered hound had attacked his small son.

The village lies in a beautiful valley, with Moel Hebog sheltering it on the west and the brooding presence of Snowdon to the north-east.

When I first heard the story of Gelert at infants' school, it made me very sad. Visit Beddgelert today and you continue to be moved by the nostalgic tale.

There are several slate quarries in North Wales that I find very impressive and are a true testimony to the toil of the workers who created them. I have visited Blaenau Ffestiniog on several occasions and have always enjoyed it. I particularly relish the train journey down to Porthmadog, on what is my favourite of the little trains of Wales. The line is Ivor the Engine country, and it is a magical journey for any child. There are those who would say that Blaenau Ffestiniog is not an attractive place, but visit it and wonder as to what went on here. Places like Blaenau show the rock that gave the people of the area their strength and character. It's no wonder that the Romans had a few problems with them. There weren't too many Roman villas around this area. Blaenau, and places like it, epitomise the homeland of North Walians. And the people include descendants of the tribes that are an essential element in the nation that is Wales. The Gogs of the north or the Hwntws of the south may keep one suspicious eye on each other – but be reassured the other eye is keeping a close watch on what is happening on the other side of Offa's Dyke to the east.

The beauty of Bodnant Gardens is enchanting. The gardens are visited by thousands each year as people make their tour of Wales. I remember the gardens because of one special man. His name was Clay Jones and he lived in the Chepstow area towards the latter end of his life. He had an impressive war record, was an expert on all gardening matters and was a regular on Radio 4's famous *Gardeners' Question Time*. As we filmed together there, the warmth of his personality came through. We filmed, as I remember, in heavy drizzle and I looked on in jealous wonder at his hair. Although we were both soaking wet, not one strand of his hair was out of place. I looked like something the cat had dragged in. Clay Jones, a wonderful man, died far too early and is greatly missed by all who knew him in Wales.

Brecon is an attractive town looking south towards the Beacons and Pen-y-Fan, the highest peak in South Wales. It has much to commend it, and its attributes are well illustrated in so many publications. My memories are entirely personal.

I was appointed to my first headship in Brecon. No, the school itself wasn't in Brecon, but the county headquarters were there at the time. It was late in 1973 and having received my headship I was due to start in April 1974, on the same day that most of the newly-reorganised counties came into being. In my case, I was to be working for Powys Education Authority. I recall the interview day very well. There must have been about 30 councillors in the chamber itself. It was quite a fair interview in that there were five questions. Most other authorities only used two questions and gave you only five minutes in which to answer both. Time was not at a premium on that day, and we were given as much time as we liked. The problem was, I felt, that two of the other candidates seemed to have a very strong chance. Many of the councillors seemed to know them. I resigned myself to being a fall guy for the day and decided I would put it down to experience. However, once the interviews were over, there was a long deliberation, and after about 45 minutes the clerk came out and asked me to re-enter the chamber. This was always a sign that you were going to be offered the job. Indeed I was, and I accepted. It was six months later before one of the county councillors felt able to tell me that there had been a problem that day, in that the voting had been split between two other candidates, and whereas neither side was able to get a majority, they decided in the end to compromise and vote for me. I was grateful for that quirk of fate; my prayer to the Almighty had not encountered an engaged signal that day.

Brynaman Baths lies alongside the pitch of the Brynaman Rugby Football Club. My first encounter with the water was when I was in the primary school. We were taken down as a class to be taught how to swim. I have to tell you that the water is not heated in Brynaman Baths, or it certainly wasn't then. You had to stand three of four yards from the rail at the side of the pool and then try to make three of four strokes to reach it before sinking. Several of us didn't make it. As I sank I remember the world turning green. Luckily the water at that end was only about three feet deep. I do feel, however, that that water was instrumental in stopping me from being any kind of choir member. It was so cold on the occasions we were there that it had an effect on our very personalities, let alone our voices. By the time we came to choose some people to be in the inter-school choir for the National Eisteddfod in Ystradgynlais in the early 1950s, my voice didn't qualify because it was entirely off the scale.

Brynaman Public Hall was my passport to the rest of the world. This is where I saw all the films in my early years. Films like *The Mudlark*, about the little boy who spent all his time on the edge of the Thames and ended up in Queen Victoria's company. When a school group were taken to see *Treasure Island*, Berian Evans hid under the seat when the nasty seaman Israel Hands chased Jim Hawkins up the rigging. Mr Jenkins, the cinema manager, always wore a suit, and had Brylcreemed hair. He was strict, and kept us all in order.

It was also a culture-led entertainment centre. The inter-chapel eisteddfod was held here once a year over three days, but I was not a great chapelgoer myself, and was disappointed not to be involved in it.

The annual local operatic society production was always an exciting time. I walked around with an autograph book, getting autographs from one or two "stars" who were ordinary people in the village, but once a year were transformed into princes in Vienna, French Legionnaires in the Sahara or students in Heidelberg.

There was once great controversy amongst the other operatic societies of the valley because Brynaman had possibly turned semi-professional, in that they had chosen a leading lady from as far afield as Clydach, 12 miles away. There was great rivalry between the operatic societies and they would come and see each other's productions each year. Bringing in performers from several miles away was really not playing the game.

Brynaman R.F.C. is situated in the old Farmers Arms in Brynaman. It's a famous place. If you have read the book *Wild Wales* by George Borrow you will know of this hostelry.

In his travels through Wales, one misty night Borrow came across the Black Mountain and down to the Gwter Fawr, the original name for Brynaman. He entered the tavern and found men around the fire drinking jugs of ale. He being a stranger, they immediately took an interest, and asked him if he had any news of the Crimean War. He had a convivial night and moved on the following day. There is now a plaque in the clubhouse which states, "George Borrow slept here."

Relatively recently an historian turned up and suggested that George Borrow didn't, in fact, sleep in that pub at all, but spent the evening and night in a pub two or three hundred yards further up the road. The club committee have considered this latest piece of news, viewed again the plaque on their own wall and quite rightly have disregarded the development. George Borrow slept there, and that's it.

My early rugby football was played at Brynaman: I played for the youth XV, the 2nd XV and the 1st XV when they were extremely short or when there was a wedding going on that particular Saturday and half the team couldn't play. When I was young and my sinews were strong and my blood was hot, Brynaman was going through a particularly lean time. In fact, the village was a dangerous place to walk about in on a Saturday morning when the team bus was roaming around looking for players. You could easily be kidnapped off the pavement to go on an away fixture, and your mother would be wondering where you were for the next few hours. On many occasions I have played on the wing for Brynaman while the bus driver played on the other wing. I didn't score many tries, although there was one ecstatic moment against Briton Ferry when I managed to get one when no one was looking. I might add, too, that when the ale is flowing and the ancients are out for an evening, one or two might still remember the pass I held against Llangennech. I was on the wing, and the centre threw a pass two yards in front of me. I stuck an arm out and the ball seemed to stick in my hand. So overcome was I with this achievement that all I could think of was to cross-kick – and then remain there in a state of wonder.

I lived here for 11 years. It was a happy home. I remember we had no furniture in one downstairs room for five years; our bathroom hung on a nail out near the back door, and our semi-detached toilets were near the one shared cold-water tap. My father worked nights regularly, so I slept with my mother until I was 10. When my father returned from night shift he would always have a warm bed to get into at eight in the morning.

In this house it always intrigued me as to the difference between women and men. When my father had a bath in front of the fire, our neighbour, Mrs Price, would often come to borrow sugar, butter or whatever. My father didn't seem to mind. He would go down in the water a little bit, for discretion's sake, but that was it. However, when Mrs Price had a bath, all doors were locked, curtains were drawn and all children sent to another street to play. Why was that, I wonder?

Upper Brynaman Junior School had burned down prior to my time there. Consequently, we were taught in temporary buildings. These buildings are still there today, but are not used as a school.

I remember when I was in Standard Two a man suddenly opened the classroom door and then apologised – he had mistaken it for a café.

I once fell from the roof of Upper Brynaman Primary School. I was taken to Morriston Hospital with a suspected fractured skull, broken leg and two broken arms. X-ray examinations confirmed only two broken wrists. What was I doing on the roof? I'm not saying.

The headmaster's study was a green shed stuck in the middle of the playground. If ever you had to report to him, it was a very long walk indeed and, on entering his domain, there was always that smell of ink, blotting paper and wet macs on rainy days.

The old Upper Brynaman Junior School, now disused.

Cader Idris is the high chieftain of Mid-Wales. It is not as high as Snowdon, but in its own way it is particularly impressive. It has great cwm or corrie basins, with steep escarpments, and one of these corries is said to be the chair of the giant Idris. According to legend, of course, anyone who spends the night on the mountain will either become a poet or a madman. I haven't had occasion to test that, but I have skirted Cader Idris many times. Now and then on these remote roads you come across a lonely telephone kiosk. I have often suggested to the BBC that we could do a programme on the kiosks of Cymru, the telephone booths of Wales. Some of them are situated in beautiful but lonely positions and it is a great source of wonder to me that you can talk to anyone from such isolated spots. But then again I still marvel at the telephone, especially when I speak quite clearly to people on the other side of the planet. I never took it for granted. As a simpleton in many ways, I'm filled with awe when I get through.

Caeo is a beautiful village just off the main road between Llanwrda and Lampeter. It's not far from Pumsaint and the Dolaucothi goldmines. We had a family attachment to Caeo because my mother's family were originally from that area.

I also remember as a little boy having two great aunts living there – Aunty Marged and Aunty Hannah. They were both married, oddly enough, to men called Dafydd. Aunty Hannah lived on a smallholding halfway between the main road and Caeo itself, and we often called there for lunch. The house was always pristine and tidy. Uncle Dafydd kept bees.

Aunty Marged was a different kettle of fish. A very colourful character, she lived next door to the Brunant Inn, in Brunant Cottage. She was worldly-wise and was very interested in politics, both local and international. She was not, however, very interested in house-keeping as such, and it was no surprise, now and again, to find magazines behind the cushions on the settee dating back to the 1930s and 1940s. However, she made a marvellous tea in the kitchen when we arrived, and I remember those occasions very warmly, especially those that ended with red jelly and Ideal Milk.

One of the downsides of visiting Caeo in my early years was discovering that not all places were on the mains sewerage system, and in both houses it was a question of a bucket out the back. Now I was not of the gentry, but I was certainly not used to that. I remember keeping my legs crossed for about eight hours on one occasion, rather than make the expedition out to the little house by the stream at the bottom of the garden.

It is amazing how images come back. I remember on one of the visits to Caeo, walking along the road after getting off the bus, and about a mile from the village seeing a rabbit that was clearly suffering from something that I was later told was myxomatosis. It was the first incident of the kind I had seen, but it stayed in the mind.

On a lighter note I remember my father telling me that he had been in the pub next door to Aunty Marged's cottage and he had been charged one shilling and sixpence for a pint, which seemed to him to be extraordinarily high. However, halfway through drinking the pint, the landlord realised that he was related to Marged next door and said "Oh, here's thruppence back – I thought you were a tourist". That was more than 40 years ago. These days, the Brunant Arms is convivial to all, and an excellent place to pull in for refreshment before continuing on one's journey.

I love Caerleon because there is a real sense of Roman history there. The fact that Britain only had three legionary fortresses, one at Chester, one at York and one at Caerleon, says a lot about the local inhabitants. The Silures tribe of South Wales, along with the others that made up what is now Wales, must have been sufficiently vigorous to have merited a full Roman legionary fortress in the region. Once, in a funeral in Maesteg, I was approached by a gentleman who suggested that the BBC should do something of a "sideline" nature about Caerleon. He said that he had researched the area on the period of the Roman occupation and found that the tribes of South East Wales had taken on the Romans in many skirmishes. As far as he could work out, by the time the Romans left, the local tribes were leading in the fixture list by something like 42 victories to 35. It was his suggestion that such facts should be put on beer mats, so that in a moment of boredom in any hostelry in the region, you could flip over a mat and there would be a piece of history to titillate your interest. Facts like: Did you know that in Fixture 22 between the Silures and the Romans, the Romans were given a good hiding and cancelled their Saturday-night orgies for the following two months?

I know that Caernarfon Castle is large, impressive, dramatic and has its own place in Welsh history, but on my visits I have also enjoyed what the harbour and the Square have to offer. I have always enjoyed the warmth of the Caernarfon welcome and I return often. I remember one incident which gave the entire area some colour. I walked into a hostelry with friends one evening and within 10 seconds of coming through the door, there was a sudden shout and a glass of ale was thrown over the head of one of the local male customers by a lady who clearly felt that he had displeased her. She then slammed the glass down on the table and stormed out. He, shouting her name, chased after her. The timing of each element of that tableau was absolutely perfect. Had it been rehearsed time and time again for television, it could not have been bettered. I do not know who she was but I felt like giving her applause for the sheer poise and vibrancy of her actions. My God, I thought, that was a six-cylinder woman.

It is an incredible thing that in all my years of going to Tenby as a young boy for holidays, I never set foot on Caldey Island. I went near it, I went around it but I never set foot on its soil. It was 1996 before I finally made a determined effort to get to the island – and I was not at all disappointed. However, as Elaine and I sat on the grass on the far side of the island, enjoying the warmth and the aerobatics of the seabirds, there was a reminder that you are never really safe anywhere. From around the corner came another couple and there was a sudden shout of "Roy, how are you?" The person had been in the same year as me in college and we hadn't seen each other for 30 years. On that day, as we were just taking the air and quietly letting the world go by, it was a sharp reminder that if you are ever up to no good, someone, somewhere will know, because Wales is a small place and it will get about sooner or later. Just beware, that's all; stay on the straight and narrow. It's easier on the blood pressure, anyway.

Oh, how I could eulogise about the occasions that I have spent in Cardiff Arms Park. I could go on at length about my experiences under the old North Stand, where, however packed in you were, if liquid suddenly leaked from the grandstand above you, somehow you still managed to make a space for whatever it was to hit the ground. Cardiff Arms Park for me, though, is a memory of how I managed to get tickets. It was a relationship I built up with Bill Clement, past WRU Secretary, and later Ray Williams, who also held the post. I started a correspondence with Bill Clement whereby I always sent him a begging letter, enclosing a stamped, addressed envelope and an open cheque made out to the Welsh Rugby Union. My ploy was that I was really asking on behalf of an uncle of mine, who had lost a leg at Dunkirk and an arm on D-Day and who was a passionate follower of the game. I did point out, of course, that if he was given a field ticket, on every occasion he got excited, he would tend to fall over unless packed closely within the ground. A grandstand ticket would be so much more comfortable for him, and as he was a gregarious man, two grandstand tickets would be even better, so that I could at least accompany him and provide a comrade for the day. Bill Clement never answered the letter but I always received the self-addressed envelope enclosing one grandstand ticket. It was a sense of achievement getting that

ticket, but all that romance and effort has now gone. It was always one-upmanship to be able to say that you knew someone, who knew someone, who knew someone, who might be able to get you a ticket. Now the distribution system and the hospitality occasions prior to the game have made it all a little banal and, dare I say it, made some of the occasions something akin to Henley, Wimbledon and Ascot. You don't really have to know what is going on as long as you are there, which is a great shame.

Cardiff Bus Station became my gateway to the capital city when I first went to college. My mother had warned me "Now you take care and keep a keen eye out for those Cardiff girls". I avidly looked out for three years, but I was never lucky in that direction. I once met a few of my co-students in Astey's cafe on the edge of the bus station and, looking through the window, I wondered where these places were that I saw on the destination boards of the buses – places like Nantyglo, Abersychan, British, Sebastopol, Oakdale, Cross Keys. They were all new places to me; I had seen a few on the map, but not all of them. I got to know the city bus routes particularly well, especially the buses running to Heath Park and to Cyncoed, where the college was situated. I vividly recall my 19th birthday, when a certain celebration had taken place. I wasn't feeling one hundred per cent as I stood at the bus stop, so I took a little walk towards the bushes of the Friary Gardens. Suddenly there was a shout to say that the bus was coming. I turned hurriedly and was about to jump on the bus when somebody said, "Where are your teeth?" I had lost my two front teeth in an accident some years previously. Where were those two front teeth? I'm tempted to say, but this is not the time.

Although Cardiff Castle is a folly in most parts and was built towards the end of the last century, it still holds a particular interest for me. It is, after all, built on the base of a Roman fort, parts of which can still be seen today. Inside its walls there is a genuine Norman keep. I have a special regard for the Banqueting Hall, which is a magnificent room with a particularly attractive ceiling. It is marvellous for a wedding reception, but as a formal dinner venue, I have found it to be a lucky place for me. I have spoken at many functions there, but I particularly recall a Cardiff Medical Society evening. I suggested in my speech that for myself, as a confirmed hypochondriac, it was a particularly safe place to be, but a surgeon quickly told me that my confidence was misplaced. If I were to collapse, there would be 120 second opinions and during the ensuing debate I would probably pass away!

What a convenient place to leap to the world – but my image of the airport includes indelible memories of two particular flights. Following our marriage, Elaine and I flew to Majorca for our honeymoon. I didn't realise at the time that the seat tickets were not numbered, so you could sit where you liked on the aircraft – and being a gentleman I allowed most of the people to get on the flight before me. Consequently I found myself going on honeymoon sitting four rows away from my bride. I made my mind up that on the return journey things would be different. A fortnight later at Palma Airport, waiting for the return flight, we sat near the door so that when the flight number was called we would be near the front of the queue – and so it proved to be. As we were led across the tarmac by an air hostess, towards the waiting Viscount, we were about four couples from the front. Suddenly a man from Bargoed began to run from the back of the queue. He had a sombrero on his head and was carrying a stuffed donkey along with two suitcases. He had decided that he wanted a good seat on the plane. One or two others decided that it wasn't such a bad idea, and they began running as well. The queue broke up. It was like a rush of refugees trying to get on the last flight out from some desperate country. The air hostess stood at the foot of the steps shouting "Back, back, you can't get on". I have to say her pleas were ignored. I must have been twentieth or twenty-first on to the aircraft – I but I am proud to say I managed to sit next to my new wife all the way home.

Elaine and I spent our wedding night here in the room above the Scholl shop in Queen Street. The room cost £6, which was an extraordinary amount in 1968, but it did have a three-piece suite, which was something special for us, let me tell you. The Scholl shop has now moved, so that I now find it difficult to pinpoint the room.

Cardiff Training College was split between two sites – at Heath Park and Cyncoed – during my time there. Roath Park Lake was midway between them. This was a wonderful place for walks and for general relaxation, and if you felt more physical, even the odd stint on the rowing boats could hone a young man's mind. I particularly liked spring, when the cherry trees were in blossom. My most vivid memories, though, are of the winter of 1962/63. It was a hard winter, and for many months the lake remained frozen solid. We were able to walk over it without any problem at all.

The Exchange Building in Cardiff Bay is a marvellous edifice. Unfortunately it was the venue of one of my most disastrous speaking engagements. It was a Round Table occasion of considerable note and spirits were very, very high indeed. The Lord Lieutenant was very fortunate. He spoke and then left because he had another engagement. By the time it came to my turn to speak, we'd already had a comfort break in which men were seen to be playing aeroplanes around the room. This involved four men holding a fifth man above them, and he, holding his arms out, would attack another so-called aeroplane coming from another direction. Had I been able to join them it might have been all right, but I was required to remain reasonably sedate prior to my speech. My effort was, to say the least, acoustically challenged. After about 10 minutes or so, one gentleman must have felt sympathy for me because a note was passed to me saying "Roy, give it up. I think the evening's over, don't you?" I readily agreed with him. In fact, I felt the evening had been over about 30 minutes before that. The host Round Table has gone from strength to strength and I wish them well, as I do all the other fraternal delegates who turned up on that occasion. It was some years ago, but I still feel the scar now, especially when I wake up suddenly in the middle of the night.

From 1961 to 1964, I was a student teacher at what was then called Cardiff Training College (now part of UWIC). Originally based in the buildings of an old Army camp in Heath Park, new college buildings were opened at Cyncoed during my time there, and I made many lifelong friends on the two sites.

The college concentrated on physical education and most of the students there, on the male side, looked like young gladiators in their green tracksuits. Of the 60 or so men in my year, well over 40 were in P.E. and the rest of us were in the general department. We were regarded in many ways as lesser beings, and on our second day there we were taken to a side room by the vice principal, who delicately suggested to us that we shouldn't bring the college into any kind of disrepute. We were a new kind of animal to his mind, and he was not used to dealing with non-P.E. types. Even our plea that we were thinkers rather than doers fell generally on deaf years. So intimidated was I that after six weeks I felt I had to change my subjects, which were originally geography and art. In the art class there were 15 women and myself; I stuck it out until we got to embroidery – and then I was gone in a cloud of dust. I changed to history, and also started studying the Rugby Football Union laws so that I could qualify as a referee. I did manage to play for the college at rugby football, but, I hasten to add, it was for the third team, and it was during a very nasty outbreak of gastro-enteritis when many of the young gladiators were unavailable for selection. To be fair to my P.E. colleagues, at the end of the first year they appointed me their student representative and at the end of the second year I became the student president. In that capacity I was able to visit many conferences throughout the land, and for the first time was able to speak publicly from various platforms.

Carreg Cennen Castle is a kind of pilgrimage centre for me. I don't know why, but once a year, when I was young, children of neighbouring villages, especially those in the Amman Valley and beyond up towards Llandybie and Llandeilo, would walk to Carreg Cennen Castle on what was Whit Monday, the old Bank Holiday at that time of the year. It was not unusual to have a hundred or more children there from the various villages, all having arrived with their old ex-Army haversacks containing their bottle of pop or water and all kinds of sandwiches, including the ones I particularly liked – those with the condensed-milk filling. Fun and games would be indulged in during the day, and all kinds of derring-do down in the dungeon as well.

In the evening, everyone would make the long trek back to their various homes. My route was over the Black Mountain. In later years Carreg Cennen became courting country for me, because I had been told by a soothsayer of the area that there's a certain romantic power about the place. If a girl cannot succumb to your charms in Carreg Cennen Castle she never will, and the relationship was never be meant to be. I confess to having tried out the potent force of the place myself – with very definite success, I might add.

As a student I had a summer job two years running with Llandeilo Rural District Council. The first year I was on the "muck gang". The second year, paid a bit more, I was on the "water gang". I remember digging a trench on the road to Cilycwm from Llandovery, having been taken there in the van in the morning. Incidentally, I think we hold the record for the number of people in a van. From that small Morris van I think eight of us emerged. I wonder if the feat is mentioned in the council archives.

I recall one particular fine day when the trench, as ever under the guidance of Trevor the Foreman from Penygroes, was alive with discussion. The debate centred on whether it was easier to do your courting in English or in Welsh. In the trench at the time was Gareth Jones, who is now the headteacher of Lampeter Comprehensive School, and Dr. John Davies, who is now the honorary physician for the Welsh Rugby Union. I was there, too, as was Bob Eak, who was a poet on a long-handled shovel. The consensus at the end of the day was that it was easier, in fact, to do your courting in English because you could take examples of telling phrases from films you might have seen in the local cinema. Therefore, you might find it easier to get across your intention and desire in that language rather than Welsh. I remember Trevor capped it all by saying that a literary knowledge of any language does not\ have to be deep and profound, because he had fought his way through the desert campaign and through Italy during World War II on just two words in various languages – "How much?"

Clarach Bay is north of Aberystwyth, beyond Constitution Hill. At the end of the promenade in Aberystwyth I used to enjoy the ride on the cliff railway, and if you make it to the top and then walk along the paths that eventually take you down to Clarach Bay you will not be disappointed. The beach is sandy and it takes you away from the bustle of Aberystwyth itself. I made that effort on a day trip in the summer of 1961; I was not alone and, ah yes, I remember it well.

I like Cowbridge, and it has been good to me. Before I was married I was appointed to Cowbridge Grammar School as a temporary teacher. I was a little reticent because I expected the school to be full of Oxbridge people and wondered whether I would be intimidated. It could not have

been further from the truth. I enjoyed my stay there immensely.

As a young buck bachelor I was often very glad of the arrangements made by the two boarding masters of the time: Wyn Oliver, who was in charge of P.E., and Iolo Davies the classics man, who was later to become

headmaster. At the time, I was staying near Crossways in very congenial digs. However, sometimes the charms of Cowbridge held me there until late into the evening. The boarding masters would always find me a spare bed, which was very kind of them, and, after all, it was a

way of keeping the bedclothes aired. The staff had many characters, one or two of whom had their own special chairs in the staff room. I remember one head of department who had a chair which he had placed in a strategic spot so that he could view his class from the staff room without the inconvenience of having to meet the class face to face. I'm not saying he did it often, but with many classes he did feel the need to slip into the staff room at regular intervals. Another head of department had a very thrifty way of filling in report forms. When it came to his section he usually found that one word would suffice; "Excellent", "Good" and "Hopeless" were three of the more frequently used adjectives.

I am going back a few years, of course, but I remember an interesting discussion on one occasion between the caretaker of the Boys' Grammar School and the caretaker of the Girls' High School before they amalgamated into the Comprehensive School. They were comparing the graffiti on the toilet walls of both schools. I have to report that the caretaker of the girls' school won hands down. There was a literary imagination displayed there that could not be matched at the boys' establishment.

If you take the road from Hirwaun that climbs away from Rhigos up over the Treherbert ridge and down towards Treherbert itself and the Rhondda Fawr valley, it is worth pulling into the lay-by, where you will usually find an ice-cream van. Immediately below you on the escarpment looking north, you will see Tower Colliery. To your left in the corrie, or cwm, you will see a lake. When the lake was enlarged at the turn of the century many Bronze Age artefacts were found, which are now in the National Museum of Wales in Cardiff. However, the interesting point about this spot is that I was once told, while refreshing myself in a hostelry in Glynneath, that the Treherbert ridge and Craig-y-Llyn in particular, had a geographical significance. The gentleman who passed on this information and who became my brief companion in the pub, told me that if you stand on that ridge and face east, then the next highest land you come to if you proceed in that direction, is the Urals of Russia. I have looked closely at a map and I think he may be right. You have the flatlands of England, then cross the North Sea, Holland, Germany, and Poland before reaching Russia and, indeed, the Urals. Can anyone verify this? If you stand on Craig-y-Llyn and look east, is the next highest point actually situated in the Urals of Russia? I need the proof, if only to satisfy my own mind.

This area of Wales is David Lloyd George's domain and I have been to the region many, many times. Although I visited Criccieth Castle only once, it left its mark on me. On my visit, it was a beautiful day and yet there was a strong, blustery wind coming off the sea. The surf was coming in in vast, impressive rollers and as I tried to get through the main gate of the castle itself, my trench coat was blown out behind me like the flag on a destroyer doing 30 knots plus. It was a day crying out for a scene from a medieval drama, but all that was on offer was me, with one hand on my cap and the other on the lapels of my coat. I spent most of my time behind a wall trying to eat my sandwiches with the wind blowing my lettuce and tomato all over the place.

I was fortunate when I was a head teacher in Powys to have been in charge of two schools in remarkably beautiful areas – Pontneddfechan and Llangattock. Across the river bridge from Llangattock is Crickhowell, a very attractive town of charm and culture, and I was privileged in arranging a contact between Crickhowell High School and a school in Baunatal, near Kassel, in Germany. I was so pleased to see that the link was enhanced by further cultural and musical relationships from within the town itself.

On the refreshment and replenishment front, the Usk Valley is fortunate in having many restful oases at which to stop. Indeed, if we still had horse-drawn carriages around the byways of the country here at the doorway of the 21st century, then I am sure they'd make huge detours just to call into places like the Bear Hotel.

Sometimes our day trips from Brynaman would take us via the Elan Valley to Aberystwyth. As the road leads west out of Rhayader towards the lakes, it then changes to a mountain road which is highly scenic. As you move on from the lovely hamlet of Cwmystwyth the landscape suddenly changes to spoil heaps and scarred hillsides. It is particularly atmospheric if you are in the area when the mist is low on the hills. Here was one of the largest lead mines in Mid Wales, first operated by the Romans but really developed in the 17th and 18th centuries. Derelict workers' buildings are still seen below the old workings. View the site from a distance because to approach it too closely might not be advisable. Coming across this site over the rolling hills of Mid Wales and the Cambrian Mountains there is a dramatic change in that it has the air of an abandoned town or village of the kind you see in America after the gold runs out and people move on. Incidentally, on one of these day trips, I remember one year there seemed to be an incident behind the bus when we had stopped for a rest in Rhayader itself. It clearly hinted at a certain scandal but to this day I have never discovered what it was. I was only 10 at the time and I wasn't privy to the tut-tutting, the raised eyebrows and dark looks. If anyone knows the story, do let me know, for I've often wondered what happened.

Cynghordy Viaduct lies on the Heart of Wales railway line. If you would like to drop off the planet and have a relaxing few hours passing through the scenery of Wales, this is the trip for you. As you travel north passing Llandeilo and Llandovery, eventually you get to Cynghordy. The viaduct itself is impressive, but if you look south down the Towy Valley, what a vista! Refreshments are available on the train, supplied by volunteers who bring their hospitality on at various stations. All power to their elbow and many thanks for their service. It is the kind of railway line that cries out for one of those observation cars they have on American trains. On the other hand there are one or two problems with bridges – ducking your head wouldn't help much at all. Each time I take a train journey, I am reminded of one I took back to Brynaman after a hot day in July on the beach at Swansea Bay. In the carriage on the way home, my auntie suddenly gave me a cwtch, not realising that I had burnt my skin badly that day. I didn't have any calamine lotion to ease the stinging sensation and I admit to a few tears after her handling.

Head for Devil's Bridge from Aberystwyth or follow the road eastwards along the ridge that looks down on the Rheidol Valley. Stop often unless you want to be a statistic, because your eyes will be drawn away from the steering wheel to the dropping landscape of the valley to the north and the rolling hills beyond. I once spent a very pleasant night in the Hafod Arms Hotel in Devil's Bridge. The bedroom was at the front of the hotel and the view was towards the gorge. It all had a vaguely alpine air about it. Oh yes, I once had an accident involving a sheep in the area, too. The sheep actually hit my car rather than the other way around. My concern for the sheep was tempered by the knowledge later that the damage to the car was £200 and I remember that the sheep had walked away in disdain.

If ever I found out in researching my family pedigree that I had a touch of blue in my blood, then I hope the line would take me to Dinefwr. It would be at the top of my list for country estates, probably because my home is not too far away and I know the area well. I think I could manage elevation to the peerage without any trouble at all. Newton House, now restored, would be a fine and fitting desirable detached residence for a Noble, I feel. I am also intrigued by the white cattle of substantial pedigree that have their home at Dinefwr. Such was their value that I believe during wartime they were camouflaged in case they were attacked from the air.

Dolgellau·is on the A470 ley line between Cardiff and Llandudno. It is a lovely town, and I rarely travel to the north without calling in. It has the kind of town square that you expect to see in places that seem to be well organised and know what they're about, and many is the time my plastic card has been grateful for the hole in the wall there.

I have also had the pleasure of staying in the town, but images of candlewick bedspreads come to mind. A certain young BBC producer had a phobia about candlewick bedspreads, and if an hotel or guesthouse used such bedding, he'd be gone in a flash. Thankfully, the rest of the team found duvets wherever they went.

At one time, this house was known as the best council house in both Mid-Glamorgan and South Glamorgan under the old county arrangements. It has a history of its own and has been famous for conferences and meetings galore over the years. For Elaine and myself, though, it was the venue of our 25th wedding anniversary celebrations, and God was in his heaven that day. The weather was fine, the locale magnificent, and the company very convivial indeed. If ever it is surplus to requirements, I would certainly put in an offer – on a rental basis only, of course.

I have skirted the Eppynt Mountain on countless occasions, travelling through Pwllgloyw, Lower Chapel, Upper Chapel and on to Builth Wells.

Sometimes my journey took me to Garth and Llanwrtyd Wells and if you take this route you cross the Army practice ranges and pass through the austere "village" built for training purposes. The lonely Drovers Inn has a particularly ghostly air about it.

I have often been regaled by Dr Elwyn Bowen, of Cefn Coed, who knows more about the Breknock region than most, with exciting tales of wartime smuggling in the area. It is said by those who know that during World War II a hearse was seen driving over the Eppynt each day. But the coffin it carried had no room for a body because it was stuffed with butter, eggs and bacon destined for the black market. I'm sure the tale is merely the stuff of legend – or is it just safer to say that?

Ferryside is a pretty Carmarthen Bay village on the east bank of the Towy estuary, just across the water from Llansteffan.

I have visited many times, but to me, Ferryside primarily means brogue shoes, the InterCity 125 and wine etiquette (grade D-minus).

Many years ago I had occasion to attend an educational course in Ferryside. It was run by Her Majesty's Inspectors and we of the headship, prospective headship, deputy-headship and prospective deputy-headship category were all crawling like mad.

I managed to leave a relatively new pair of brogue shoes at the educational centre, and to this day they are missing. I was also intrigued to see the Carmarthen-London InterCity 125 stop at Ferryside Station. It smacked of the old days when trains didn't ignore any station at all, and to see the London-bound express pull to a halt there

restored my faith in equality for the people.

When the course was over, the week ended with an evening of entertainment. I was elected compere for the unofficial concert and I was asked to sit with H.M. Inspectors. I thought, "Hey, I'm well in here, my promotion is obviously imminent."

But when the adrenalin is flowing and the mood of the moment becomes intoxicating, sometimes, just sometimes, you're digging for yourself a sizeable hole.

Following the introduction of an act, with a funny story added for good measure, I would return to the table and take a large slurp of the wine from the nearest glass. The trouble was the nearest glass was, invariably, not mine, and by the end of the evening I had been found to have been drinking from four of the inspectors' glasses in all. Things went quiet on the promotion front for a while.

What an attractive small fishing harbour and famous, of course, for the filming of *Moby Dick*. I have not visited Lower Fishguard as often as I have visited Fishguard merely because the latter is a gateway to the west and Ireland, but all the trips I have taken have been very pleasant. There was one day in Fishguard itself though, many years ago, when we stopped for some refreshment. It was in the 1960s and we went towards a cafe when I saw a sign on the door which said "Closed for lunch". I looked around for the *Candid Camera* people but, no, it appeared to be true. It reminded me of a taxi firm I once came across in North Wales. I won't be specific as to where it was, but there was an advertisement on the side of the taxi which said "Open 24 hours from 9am."

It's a strange thing, but they appear as if from nowhere, these Glantawe Coaches. They seem to follow me and seek me out. I have been in lonely parts of the United Kingdom, in far-flung corners of Europe, when suddenly from around a corner comes a Glantawe Coach. It's uncanny, and in the end we have built up a relationship over which neither of us, the coach or myself, has any control. It's destiny that we continue to meet, somewhere, sometime.

The Gliffaes Hotel is near Crickhowell. I include it because it has a romantic air as soon as you see it.

On the first occasion that I visited it, snow lay on the ground and, immediately, I was thrown back to a vision of a scene in *Dr. Zhivago*. Being a romantic at heart, it was a film that I loved and when I saw Gliffaes on that day it was like a time warp that had thrown the Steppes of Russia at the beginning of this century deep into Powys and the Usk Valley. Anyway, I have to confess to having a weakness for any large building which has a tower to it or any section resembling a tower. I don't know what it is but I have always coveted places with towers. I suppose some psychologist would be able to explain it as a Noble subconsciously seeking out his castle.

Gwaun Cae Gurwen, or the Waun as we knew it, was a great attraction on a Saturday night. It had the cinema where you could do your courting just outside your own village, and the tale of your derring-do might not get back to your home patch. After the early show on a Saturday night you also had time to continue your courting down by the viaduct. The viaduct was quite unique. It was built to carry a railway line, but the line was never built. I remember as a little boy crossing it with my family to visit an aunty who lived on the mountain on the other side of the valley, and looking down giddily at the river below. In my courting days, you had to go down under the viaduct quite early to get a place.

Gwaun Cae Gurwen also gave me early experience of the "monkey parade", walking along Gwaun Cae Gurwen Common, boys on one side and girls on the other, just to see if a passing interest and attraction developed into something more. That was where I first showed off my new, shiny-green trenchcoat. It had buckles everywhere and was quite, quite magnificent. It was a class above the duffel coats which were in vogue at the time and was a real conversation stopper on the Common.

Gwawr Chapel at Godreaman, Aberdare, is the chapel where Elaine worshipped and where we married in 1968. When the original Gwawr Chapel was demolished as unsafe, the Welsh Baptists of the area took over the vacant Hebron Chapel and re-named it. The problem was that no one remembered to re-register it as a place of marriages. When that realisation dawned on us, there were some fast and frantic re-arrangements made with the registrar during the week prior to the wedding. Good heavens! Our marriage was almost illegal, and that would never have done. After all, Elaine's father had been a deacon at Gwawr.

The small village of Gwynfe lies on a hill just off the road between Brynaman and Llangadog. My family visited there when we went to Ysguborwen Farm, where one branch of our family lived. Indeed, I think the family, third generation, still have responsibility for the farm.

At the time we visited, Aunty May lived there with Uncle James, who seemed to me a formidable character. Apparently he had been married three times altogether and had one leg. I was told that he lost the leg in a threshing machine, which to me made him quite an extraordinarily brave and charismatic man. As far as I was concerned, he might have lost it at Waterloo; it had that same kind of romance about it.

In the farmhouse fireplace the big cauldron, the crochan, always held gently-steaming cawl. I must have been going through a funny phase in that I was finicky with my food for a couple of years and I remember being offered rabbit for dinner. I didn't fancy that at all – I ended up having a boiled egg.

The New Inn provided me with a good lay-by during courting days, but my association goes back further than that to our family visits to Gwynfe and Ysguborwen Farm. We travelled on the Thomas Bros. buses which came to Brynaman on Tuesdays and Fridays. They dropped us off at New Inn, and then we had to walk past Jerusalem Chapel, up the hill and on to the farm.

In the evening when the visit was over my Aunty May would arrange for a car to come and get us from a house near New Inn. The cars were based there and were usually used for funerals, but were also used as a connecting service from outlying farms to the bus that took us back over the mountain.

In later years, the New Inn was a favourite watering hole for Elaine and myself to do our courting. It was a warm cosy pub, and there was a colourful character called "Madam" who ran the place. Sadly, it's a pub no longer.

Crimea Pass

Horseshoe Pass

I include these because they have such evocative names, conjuring up images of dramatic landscape and wild remoteness. They almost invite an expedition to answer their challenge.

Actually, in winter they regularly add drama to the weather forecasts, when the road over one, or both, will be closed because of snow.

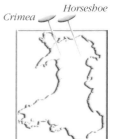

Crimea *Horseshoe*

Laugharne, beautiful Laugharne. I suppose Laugharne is synonymous with Dylan Thomas, but it goes back way, way beyond Dylan – to the time of the medieval knights when the Normans were in the area. Once a year, even now, the local inhabitants will beat the bounds, or walk the boundaries of the land that they were given by the sitting tenant in Laugharne Castle so many centuries ago.

I think of Laugharne, though, on two personal levels. One is that whenever I have visited Dylan's Boat House I have been given a warm welcome by the ladies who work there. There is always a cup of coffee or tea and wonderful scones to be had on the patio, and if you are very lucky you'll just catch the tide coming in like a mini Severn Bore and setting the waiting boats a-bobbing.

The second is the Portreeve's breakfast – now there's an occasion! I was once invited as guest speaker. It happens in October each year when all the men congregate at the local primary school for breakfast. It's mostly salad, something you would expect of a lunchtime, but it's a marvellous meal, served by the women of the town. After breakfast, there are the speeches – usually two – before the men walk down to the Town Hall, where a quick prayer is said, and then they all march on to the church. There, a service lasts an hour or so, and they all march back again for another prayer outside the Town Hall. After that, the pubs are visited, particularly Brown's Hotel, famous for hosting Dylan Thomas's drinking. It is an arduous day for the constitution, but one that remains in the memory for all the right reasons.

I was never one to take the waters at Llandrindod Wells, but I did come across the town in my professional capacity in education. It is close to my heart because I received my second headship from Powys County Council at a meeting in County Hall in Llandrindod Wells. It is odd the things you remember, for the applicants of the day were allowed some time off during proceedings and we all walked around the lake in the park. I saw an elderly man and a young boy, fishing. I took them to be grandfather and grandson. They had caught a very big fish which lay on the path just alongside the lake itself. As they congratulated

themselves and prepared to put the catch in the bag, the fish suddenly came to life, bounced and went back into the water. I thought that they took the disappointment very well.

Later on in County Hall at the interview itself, I had occasion to go to the men's room. There I saw six councillors huddled together in animated conversation. They were clearly talking about the attributes of the candidates. As I came in all went quiet, five of them left and I found myself alongside the remaining one, he in one trough, me in the other. We had a bizarre conversation whilst facing the wall, he suggesting that if I performed as well in the second interview then there was every chance of me getting the job. I thanked him profusely and avoided the temptation to shake his hand, bearing in mind that we were in a male urinal and I didn't want to be seen ingratiating myself to a councillor on such a day. After all, the application form did include the statement "canvassing councillors is disallowed and will result in disqualification of the candidate".

Llandudno's beautiful bay neatly fills the gap between the Great Orme and Little Orme. For me, the resort has carved a niche for itself on memory levels far beyond the tourist trail.

I regularly visited Llandudno as a headteacher in charge of children on educational visits to North Wales. It was our base for trips to Snowdonia, Llechwedd Slate Caverns, Betws-y-Coed and beyond.

It was also our base when we took the Ystradgynlais and District Under-11 rugby side on northern expeditions. One year we had three Ystradgynlais R.F.C. "Glyns" in support – Glyn, Chairman; Glyn, President; and Glyn, Treasurer. Our group was split between two hotels and on one strategically-planned evening we shared a drink in one hotel and afterwards accompanied the Glyns to theirs. On arrival there, we shared another convivial slurp and they insisted that they accompany us back to our hotel. Then, after suitable refreshment, we formed an escort for them on their return journey. This inter-hotel accompanying arrangement went on for three hours!

Llangattock Ridge is a dramatic escarpment overlooking the village of Llangattock and Crickhowell. It's an extraordinary thing that I have spent most of my life on or near limestone. In Brynaman, my home village, there is a limestone ridge that forms part of the Black Mountain. It stretches eastwards to go through Penderyn, where there is a limestone quarry, not far from where I live at present, and Llangattock is the village in which I was the head teacher for five years. I seem to be drawn to limestone. The escarpment is famed for its cave systems, which should be entered only by experienced cavers. The ridge forms a barrier between industrial South Wales and the Usk Valley with Mid Wales beyond. Indeed the difference in geography is very dramatic.

On many a morning as I drove to work, I would come to the ridge overlooking the Usk Valley and see thick cloud lying at its base, like a smooth white lake. Each hill and mountain stood above it like islands in a white sea. Sometimes I was late leaving Llangattock School because of a governors meeting, and on one such occasion as I drove up from the village towards Beaufort I came across an extraordinary scene. The Falklands War was at its height then, and up on the ridge a night war-game was going on between two forces of Gurkha troops. Jeeps with coloured flags carried umpires who had the last word as to who was "dead" or "injured". Helicopters without lights hovered above the ridge. I have to say that had I been captured, I would have told them everything that I knew and then some.

I have visited Llangollen many times on the occasion of the International Eisteddfod and the sheer bringing together of so many representatives from different countries around the world is an inspiring sight in itself. It is such a huge Welsh step towards tolerance, mutual appreciation and an inter-mingling of cultures. The International Eisteddfod stands as one of the true great events of Wales and flies our flag throughout the world. How many people will return home, successful or otherwise, and speak warmly of our country? Thousands upon thousands, I'm sure. It is such a marvellous initiative and its importance cannot be over-emphasised.

Not far from Brecon is Llangorse Lake, where evidence of ancient habitation has been found. As proof of my ability to rough it, this was the site of my one and only experience of camping. I spent the night there with the boys of Cowbridge Grammar School who were on a camping course while I was teaching at the school. The groundsheet was certainly waterproof, but it didn't have an air cushion. Consequently, I woke up in the morning as stiff as a board and my efforts to get to the ablutions through the early-morning mist rising off the lake would clearly define me as a non-Tarzan type, and on any mountaineering course I would probably get a D-minus.

I remember a query I once put out on the radio programme, asking which was the exact mid-spot of Wales. I think it is somewhere in the Cambrian Mountains, not far from Cader Idris. But a very good candidate, in terms of villages, is Llangurig. On the journey from South Wales to North Wales, when you reach Llangurig you do feel as if you are getting somewhere, and if you also feel like refreshment, I recommend you pull in away from the by-pass and stop awhile, for there is a very good place there for a cup of tea and a cake. It's an old vicarage and you'll find it easily.

Llantwit Major was on my prolonged supply-teaching route when I first returned from England after doing my missionary work teaching in the Bath area. I taught at St. Illtyd's Primary School, which catered for children at the RAF Station at St. Athan. I had the good fortune to stay with one of the characters of the town. Her name was Mrs Mary Pearce and she lived in The Curriers, a disenfranchised pub from decades previously. Mrs Pearce provided bed and breakfast and I stayed with her for six months. She was a woman of substance, who took her baths once a week in a tin tub out in the old stable, which had doors on one end and a gap which should have had a door in the other end. The Curriers is situated in old Llantwit Major, which is a very picturesque small town. Mrs Pearce was hardy and welcoming, taking a bottle of Mackeson most evenings and a hearty breakfast each morning.

I have to confess that I have had three periods of hypochondria in my life and the first one I experienced in Llantwit Major. As I lay in bed at night, if I wanted to visit the "comfort cabin", it was at the bottom of the garden. It was quite a long journey which required you to put on six different light switches before you even got to the back door, and a cold night in January discourages that kind of journey anyway. In bed one night, for some reason I felt unnaturally cold. I had read somewhere that being very, very cold is one of the most comfortable ways to die and you have to be careful about letting yourself slip away. I put on a vest under my pyjamas, a tracksuit, a pair of rugby socks, a Dai cap, a pair of gloves and a scarf. I also ripped some pages out of holiday brochures to stick in the window just in case there might be a draught coming through, even though I couldn't feel it. I began to have aches and pains everywhere over the next few weeks and I visited the doctor. It was the first time for me to encounter an appointment system, so it was a world first. He checked me over and could not find anything wrong at all – in fact he suggested that I had too many pains in too many places for it to be serious. He asked whether anything unusual was due to happen to me in the next few months. "Marriage," I said. "Ah," he said, "there we have it, you see – a change of life. Your mind is preparing for that, and your body is trying to keep up with your mind. I can assure you that once your marriage has taken place all will be back to normal again and life will be bliss." And so it proved to be. I have had two periods of hypochondria since – and I have enjoyed all three so far.

St Illtyd's Primary School

Betws, Ammanford

Looking over Crickhowell towards the Sugar Loaf

Black Rock Sands at sunset

Penarth Pier

Llanwonno Church

Anglers at Llyn Trawsfynydd

The old Severn Bridge

The Old Rectory, Rhossili Downs

Sheep on the Beacons

I have always been enthralled by the tale of Guto Nyth-brân, the athlete of old who was supposed to have been able to run from Llanwonno Church to Mountain Ash in the time it took a kettle to boil. Sadly, his love of running proved the death of him – he collapsed and died in 1737 just as he was being congratulated on covering the 12 miles from Newport to Bedwas Church in 53 minutes.

Llanwonno is a fine place to visit anyway, especially in autumn, when the area rivals the Forest of Dean for colour and pre-winter hues among the tree-clad hills. At Llanwonno itself there is a church and a pub, but its quiet loneliness has real appeal.

There are two lakes with this name – Llyn-y-Fan Fawr and Llyn-y-Fan Fach.

Llyn-y-Fan Fach is an enchanting place. Travel to Llanddeusant and take your car into the hills, but only so far, because you eventually have to leave it and continue on foot. The walk is well worth the effort, for this is a place of myth and magic.

Llyn-y-Fan is the home of the legend of the Lady of the Lake. It is quiet, it is still, and as legend will tell you it is supposed to be a place where no birds sing. I don't know whether that is true or not, but I've been there four or five times and I've yet to hear my first tweet.

Indeed, if you stand there and close your eyes, you can well imagine a lady coming out of the water and entrancing you, as she did so many hundreds of years ago, to a farmer who was busily going about his business, but hadn't fully appreciated that it would be a day slightly different from all the rest. Having married him, and having eventually returned to the lake under the conditions she laid down for him, legend tells of the mark of a plough, made as his cattle dragged the implement towards the water as they, too, disappeared below the surface. I walked around the lake three times; I still didn't find the plough mark.

I cannot think of Margam Park without thinking of the the Women's Institute, but let me first put the place into context.

The park is a beautiful rural oasis to the east of Port Talbot and the grandeur of the main house, with the impressive flight of steps leading up to it, gives an immediate impression of being in a fine country estate. The elegant and famous orangery is an asset that lends itself so easily to any function or event that is based in Margam.

I am a great fan of the WI and I have attended many of their functions. Some years ago I was due to open a large WI jamboree at the park and as I queued in a line of vehicles near the entrance, my car was suddenly hit by the one behind.

It turned out to be driven by the WI Driver of the Year. Embarrassment? Yes – but laughter, too.

The village of Meifod lies in the beautiful valley of the Afon Vyrnwy. There was a story at one time that Manchester University wished to place in the valley a massive radio-telescope of the kind they have at Jodrell Bank. Although I am in favour of scientific advancement it never came to fruition and I am glad the valley was able to remain as it was. I have visited the village many times and enjoyed the experience on every occasion. If ever you are in the area, just to the north-west of Welshpool, be sure to visit it; you will be impressed by the beauty of the landscape. Indeed, unlike valleys which are relatively wide and look neat in landscape, the valley floor itself is quite flat and the hills on either side form a boundary of the kind you'd find in a geographic model.

The tiny hamlet of Melin-y-Wern has had quite a fight to prove its existence. For years, maps did not mark it.

Near Nannerch, an attractive village not far from Mold, it is an hospitable oasis. Try the comfortable Old Mill as an overnight stop, with a call at the Cherry Pie next door for sustenance.

You could also call at the pub and craft shop – and then you would have that "I will call at Melin-y-Wern again" feeling as you journey on.

I went through a phase once of going out for a drink with the boys on a Friday night to Merthyr Tydfil.
Fridays in Merthyr were quite lively as I remember, but to me Merthyr has always been a special place.
In Welsh industrial history it has been a catalyst. Once the largest town in Wales, it was a cauldron of
activity and was a kind of Klondike to all those people who came in from so many different areas.
Merthyr Tydfil and Rhondda are names that are known worldwide and if you visit them, you will find
the people are a special breed.

I don't know whether I should mention Mwnt because it is such a private, lovely place. Where is it? It's almost a secret, but it lies somewhere between Fishguard and New Quay. There is a lovely white-washed church almost on the headland, and someone sent me a model of the building before I ever visited Mwnt. It is a place of sea, sand, solitude and absolute serenity. There is nothing there, but everything – and the small white church, of course – for those who might be after some contemplation as well as sheer contentment.

Those who take the road south from Caernarfon and head for Llanberis and Snowdon will appreciate the dramatic grandeur of the mountain lands of Wales, but for me Nant Ffrancon, south of Bethesda, is one of Snowdonia's wildest and most rugged valleys. Here are Llyn Ogwen, Llyn Bochlwyd and Llyn Idwal, guarded by Tryfan, Glyder Fach and Glyder Fawr. This is Wales at its defiant best.

Neath Gardens hold a special place in my memory, because as students returning to Cardiff Training College in the early sixties, we always got off the Western Welsh bus in Neath to switch to a Neath & Cardiff coach. Now the Western Welsh bus actually carried on to Cardiff as well, but we felt that N & C was a plusher ride. I recall the occasion when Mari from Barry Training College sat on my lap. Well, after all, the bus was very, very crowded. She was a very good hockey player, incidentally.

When shopping, if my mother couldn't get anything she wanted in Swansea, the next port of call was Neath. My main recollection of Neath is the Market, with those little places at the back where you could buy faggots and peas followed by tart and custard. You can still go and enjoy them today.

But I have one disturbing image of the town – and it's really not Neath's fault, because it was an image that I picked up in Swansea, Port Talbot and other towns, too. One or two of the shops would have school uniform in the window, quite early in the summer. I never thought that was fair. It was too early in the year and put undue pressure on the children. I always thought that children should go into the summer holidays in a happy and excited state of mind, but once I saw a school uniform in the window, I knew September and the start of a new school year couldn't be too far away.

An attractive town on the west coast along the necklace of Cardigan Bay, New Quay can lay claim to being the true Llareggub, the famous small town in Dylan Thomas's *Under Milk Wood*. Certainly, it "tumbles down to the sea" as he describes. I won't enter the debate as to whether New Quay, Laugharne, or any kind of amalgam of towns is truly Llareggub, but I will say that New Quay has featured heavily in the very few caravan holidays that I have taken. I was in my teenage years and a friend of mine, whose parents had a shop, also had a caravan in the town. Now I have always been a great harbour-watcher, envying those who had boats, yachts and big cruisers. I have never done anything about it but I have just sat on the harbour wall looking down at men and women who go "messing around in boats" and in many ways I was jealous. I just have this awful suspicion that I wouldn't be very good at it, that's all. I do confess with some shame, however, to a feeling of satisfaction many years ago when I watched one pompous yacht owner sail into the harbour and hit a submerged anchor. I felt a certain pang of sympathy for him until he managed to do it three times in the same day. The odds against him coming into the harbour on that particular tack, and in that particular direction, three times on the trot must have been enormous – but he managed it all right, and on the third occasion he did manage to succeed in putting a hole in the hull. I do envy those who are good at sailing, but deep down I just know I am a cruise-ship man myself, passing the days in a cabin with full en-suite facilities on a sea so becalmed that my gin and tonic isn't shaken at all.

For a period of my life I did try rugby refereeing. Well, if you are not much good as a rugby player, what else can you do? Many incidents during my brief period as a custodian of rugby laws come to mind, but I'll relate just the one. For many years, New Tredegar only had a youth XV and I was refereeing one morning in a fixture against Slough Colts. It was the morning of an international match in Cardiff, so the kick-off was quite early. It was pouring with rain and New Tredegar Youth were well into the lead. Just five minutes into the second half, with New Tredegar having just scored another try and while I was waiting for the conversion kick, there was a shout from the touch line. It was one of the committee men. I asked "What's the matter?" and he replied, "Ref – the ladies say the chicken and chips have arrived early, do you think you can come off now?" So we had a brief conference, the two captains and myself, and we agreed to end the game there and then. Thirty minutes first half, five minutes second half. Later that morning I hitched a lift on the team bus as it travelled down to the match in Cardiff. I was sitting in the front of the bus, but most of the players, of course, were towards the middle and the back. During the journey a bottle was passed down to me with a message, "Would you like a drink, Ref?" Now I had no real idea as to what was in it, but to my credit I did not refuse the kindly gesture and I took a hearty swig. It was bitter ale, thank heavens.

On the way to St. David's from Haverfordwest, the road dips down to Newgale Beach. It's a long stretch of sand with an adjacent bank of pebbles that tries with varying degrees of success to protect the main road from the elements. It's a refreshing place to stop on your journey westward.

On our school Arts Society trip to St. David's there was a girl who held a certain interest for me, so the "comfort break" at Newgale allowed me a chance to make a tentative move, just to test the water. As we walked along, in a group, we came to several small pools of sea-water. One was directly in our path, and it was there that I did my Sir Walter Raleigh bit and put down my coat. I said, "Here we are, don't get your feet wet, just step on my cape". She did. The state of the black zipped jacket with tartan lapels took some explaining when I got home.

Much of the dyke that King Offa built over 1200 years ago to keep the Welsh in their place can still be seen today. In 1997 the BBC decided to make a series of programmes to celebrate the history of the border itself and I was privileged to present one of them. Unbelievably, we covered 2000 years of history in just half an hour. The highlight of the filming for me was the afternoon we spent on Offa's Dyke. We were on the rampart just a few miles north of Kington and the weather played its part in adding atmosphere to the dramatic landscape about us. It was a bright, sunny, wintry day with a strong wind blowing from the west and snow to be seen on the rolling hills all around. I couldn't help thinking that it must have been an awesome sight for those living in the east when a band of wild Welsh day-trippers came over the top all those centuries ago, looking for the nearest Saxon take-away. Beef, mutton and pork were taken in that order of priority.

I first came across Ogmore Residential
Centre when, as a teacher, I went there on
a rugby coaching course under the
direction of Ray Williams, who was the
coaching guru for the WRU. Now Ogmore,
for those who know it, is a fresh place,
where no self-respecting germ is allowed
to survive. As I stood on the windswept
field in my pristine tracksuit and shining
rugby boots, the wind whipped in from
the channel and it is an extraordinary fact
of life for me to suddenly realise that
whenever I stand against the elements, the
wind is always, always, blowing across my
parting. Many years later my son was to go
to Ogmore Residential Education Centre
with the Mid Glamorgan Youth Orchestra.
What a fine organisation that was and
what a pity the counties' reorganisation
put such a facility, amenity and service for
the children under threat.

Onllwyn lies on the road between Glynneath and Abercraf on the moorland at the top of the Dulais Valley. I used to pass through it when I journeyed from Aberdare to Brynaman on regular visits to my parents.

Onllwyn has a Roman fort. I often wonder how Roman soldiers would have felt if their National Service papers landed on their mat and told them that they had been posted to Onllwyn, because it has a climate somewhat different from Rome. I have always found the people of Onllwyn and the area particularly warm, but anyone coming up from the Mediterranean area wearing a skirt as part of the uniform would find the climatic change a little uncomfortable.

Areas such as the Dulais Valley have played an important part in Welsh industrial history. It is inspiring to learn that the University of Wales, Swansea, has established a University in the Community initiative in the Onllwyn area.

During my holidays in Tenby as a boy, I often saw the big Sunderland flying boats as they skirted the town having lifted from the Haven. They were based at Pembroke Dock, and I insisted on one holiday that my parents take me by bus to see them on their home patch. Pembroke Dock has another association with my family as well, because my father was born here.

When I returned from England after my supply-teaching there, I found myself in a state of "have chalk will travel", and Penarth was one pin on my personal map. There are tales told about Penarth that suggest it is rather a snobbish place. I never found it so. The schools at which I taught in Penarth were always happy, convivial places but I do remember that in the old Penarth Grammar School there were two staff rooms, male and female, and the males went out on a Christmas "do" on their own. They did not invite the women. There was also a kind of druidic circle, to which I and another new teacher were entered at Christmas time in a pub in Penllyn. The archdruid was from the maths department and we were all given a bardic name. At the end of the ceremony we had to kneel before the archdruid who had the head of a bear hanging from a ribbon around his neck, Penarth being the Welsh for "head of the bear". At the end of his eulogy to both of us he handed the head of the

bear towards me and then said
"You are now known as Roy
Ddu – Black Roy from the Black
Mountain – and you may now
kiss my arth". I duly did, and the
bear's head was then passed on
to the other new member.
Penarth holds another memory
for me, too.

When Elaine and I celebrated
our first wedding anniversary it
was in a restaurant in the town.
It was a very fine meal, and a
marvellous occasion, but it was
the first occasion that our joint
meals had crossed the £10
barrier. We agreed not to tell our
parents about the cost, out of
sheer embarrassment. Such was
my naïvety that when the head
waiter asked me if I wanted
some extra vegetables with the
steak, I asked him what was
available, and he suggested that I
might wish to try the petits pois.
I found later that the steak
actually came with some peas,
so when the other peas came as
well there were so many that
they had to be put on a side
plate. I was able to go home
under my own steam that night.

For many people, when they think of slate quarries in North Wales, names like Blaenau Ffestiniog readily come to mind, but as you travel through Bethesda, going south, you become conscious of the massive quantities of roofing materials which have been taken from this land. The great terraces carved from the mountainside are a memorial to generations of quarrymen.

Telford's Pontcysyllte Aqueduct is a triumph of Industrial Revolution engineering. It carries the Llangollen branch of the Shropshire Union Canal and it is a bizarre sensation to float serenely on a canal boat, 120 feet above the River Dee, with very little room for your dog to go walkies on either side.

Photograph courtesy of Bridgend C.B.C.

Porthcawl was the place I visited most often as a youngster and I really loved it. The bus park in Coney Beach hasn't changed much in all these years, and neither has the fair or the seafront. I never really fancied the donkey rides, but I felt it was necessary because it was part of the tradition. I mean, I didn't mind the donkeys, they were quite nice as donkeys go, but after they had walked down to a particular spot on the beach, they always galloped back. It was that gallop that upset me, because I never quite got my feet in the stirrups.

Why hadn't they invented big beach towels then? Our towels were small red-and-white striped things. They hid nothing.

It was many years before we actually hired deck-chairs. Most years we just sat on the beach itself. When we did hire deck-chairs it was with a group of other people, and the chairs would be placed in a semi-circle so that the children could be kept in a kind of corral. I enjoyed the beach, the ride on that little train that went along the Prom for so many years, and the fairground, of course. I loved the water chute and an attraction called Over the Falls. Here, you climbed steps and sat on a long seat in a darkened room. Suddenly, the wall in front of you opened, the seat collapsed, and you found yourself being carried on a giant canvas carpet 20 feet wide over giant rollers – and, just as if you were being swept over a waterfall, you had no control of your posture. You paid sixpence for that, but you could also pay thruppence just to see other people coming Over the Falls. It was particularly interesting when girls came down – skirts were in total disarray and allowed a young man's education to be advanced somewhat as he took in the sight.

Photograph courtesy of Bridgend C.B.C.

Portmeirion is a marvellous wonderland of a village. To call it a folly would be . . . folly.
It is imagination unleashed, and Clough Williams-Ellis did what I most admire in people – tore up the established rule book to look at things anew.
His creation is a joyful jumble guaranteed to give a lecturer in the history of architecture apoplexy.
The place is enchanting, and I have made myself a promise to stay at the hotel on the water's edge for at least one night. I hope the Peacock Room is still available when I call. Viewing the estuary of Traeth Bach while in your pyjamas and contemplating a full Welsh breakfast is a wonderful way to lift the human spirit at the challenge of a new day.

I remember Pumsaint for two reasons. Once when working for the BBC we were doing a road show from Dolaucothi, the Roman goldmines, and we stayed in the Dolaucothi Arms in the village.

My bedroom was at the back of the building, and looking out of the window at night the stars were shining brightly, but there was no moon, and I had really forgotten until then how dark a country night can be.

Growing up in the city can sometimes rob you of the appreciation of the heavens. It was dark, it was still, and it was very, very silent.

On another occasion, as a student, I was working with a Llandeilo Rural District Council team digging a trench in the vicinity. The trench was deep and the day warm and sunny. Suddenly, about mid-afternoon, even though there wasn't a cloud in the sky, one of the boys said "Can you hear thunder?" I said "No". We all looked above the edge of the trench and there he was, a bull thundering down upon us from the field. I have been told that bulls have difficulty in running downhill, but clearly this bull didn't know that theory. It's a pity really that the Olympic Games selection team were not in the area at the time because I cleared that six-bar gate in the vertical position, no problem whatsoever.

Pwlldu Bay and Pwlldu Head lie between Caswell Bay and Three
Cliffs Bay.

The road to Pwlldu Head is quite narrow, but is well worth
making the effort, especially in my case, because romance is
attached to the story.

To put it into context, there are on the Garw River in Brynaman
two deep pools, both of which are called Pwlldu – the Black
Pool. There's the Upper Black Pool and the Lower Black Pool,
so this name on the Gower, I felt, had a certain
relevance for Elaine, my wife,
and myself.

It was there we got engaged. Oh yes, I did it
quite properly, formally asking for her hand in
marriage, although it had been decided
several months beforehand that this was to
be. We ended the day with a fine meal in
an hotel that is no longer there – the
Caswell Bay Hotel. We had beef with all
the trimmings. It was a good day.

There's a telephone kiosk at Pyle Square that played a part in changing my life. I had been teaching for only three years when I began to think that my life had been very confined in experience and restricted in vision. After all, I went to school when I was four years old, I stayed in school until I was 18, I then went to college and I was back in school by the time I was 21. There just had to be another life out there.

An advertisement in *The Western Mail* confirmed my suspicion that there was a world beyond the blackboard, chalk and daily register. It read "Plant Manager required for a concrete company. Salary £1,004, plus company car. Training will be given to the suitable candidate." This was it . . . my conveyor belt to the sherry and vol-au-vents crowd.

An interview was arranged and on the appointed day I drove east on the A48 (this was in pre-M4 days, you understand). As I approached Pyle my moment of destiny came upon me. There were two loud bangs and the car lurched to one side – I had suffered a double puncture.

There was drizzle in the air but I made my way towards Pyle on foot. In the telephone kiosk on the square I made my excuses to the concrete company and felt that they, at least, seemed to sympathise with my plight.

On putting the telephone down I turned to the door . . . and there he was. The Good Lord had clearly decided that my time had not yet come in the teaching world, and He had sent His messenger to stop me in my tracks.

The messenger was dressed in a heavy overcoat, scarf and a flat Dai cap, and his eyes were disconcertingly close together. He leaned on the door of the kiosk and refused to let me out. My growing frustration did not attract the attention of any passers-by, and I was in the kiosk for fully 20 minutes. Such was my flustered state when I finally emerged that I decided to contact the R.A.C. and just sit in my car to calm myself. I didn't telephone the R.A.C. for quite some time because I was afraid that the mad messenger would trap me again.

I never made it to the interview and so I missed the chance of getting to the big time in concrete. God moves in strange ways indeed when you're not playing ball in the grand scheme of things.

Rhandirmwyn is near the massive Llyn Brianne reservoir. It is a romantic place, wild and remote, and the cave that was the hide-out of Twm Shôn Catti is still there to be seen under a craggy hummock near the river. I don't know why, but I have always had a lot of time for a romantic rogue. One tends to have an image of an exciting figure, a ladies' man, caring not a jot for authority and always a banner-carrier for the little man. The truth was probably far removed from that. Such characters probably robbed from the rich and didn't give too much to the poor, and if they were alive today there would probably be a three-way split – some for themselves, some for the poor and some for the Cayman Islands account.

The Gower Peninsula ends in the wide arc of Rhossili Bay and the challenge to the sea that is Worms Head. Halfway along the bay you will find a house, at one time a rectory. It is said to be haunted, and if you walk along the shore and dare to look back upon the house, the resident spectre will be seen. I have not tested this tale of old, but such stories always intrigue me. When I was a young boy, we lived next door to a man of – how shall I put it? – varying interests. He went through a phase of spiritualism and one evening he invited our family in to a seance when he would make the small front-room table rise into the air. I was too young to be included, and to this day I'm not sure whether he was successful in his venture. Not that I believe in such things, of course!

This is the only photograph of a person that I have included in this book. Rhydwen Williams was a six-cylinder man. He was an eisteddfodic poet, an author, a preacher, a broadcaster and one of the truly great characters of Wales. His voice had a charismatic power and flow that enthralled audiences, mellowed men and disarmed women wherever he went.

In his latter years we became firm friends, the kind of bonding that knows no logic or reason, for we were different as individuals but close as true comrades.

Twice a week I visited him when he was bedridden following a stroke, but his indomitable nature was always aflame as we shared chat, argument, stories and many, many glasses of the water of life to sustain the spirit.

Rhydwen died in the same week that I completed this book. The ache of loss is immeasurable for, although he was not of my blood, yet he was of my kin. God, I will miss him. His spark of faith and vibrant life will always be with me. I hope some of his being has rubbed off on me. My one regret is that I did not meet him earlier in my life.

What an annual agricultural extravaganza the Royal Welsh Show has become.

I am usually based there with the BBC, and as my radio programme starts relatively early, I am privy to the Show as it wakes up of a morning.

Each year I learn something more, and I'm gradually becoming an agricultural groupie. The Royal Welsh, however, is far more than an agricultural show; it is a massive event and a great annual meeting place for so many. It is, I'm sure, the best show of its kind in Britain, if not Europe. The organisers couldn't possibly say that – but I can.

I long to become a member of one of the attending societies, possibly the Welsh Black Society. Each morning I pass their tent, where members can call in for breakfast. Oh, how the smell of bacon, egg, and sausage with all the trimmings can distract a man as he makes his way to work of a morning!

Sarn Helen is a Roman road that runs through Wales, and one section goes from Neath to Brecon, passing Onllwyn and moving to skirt Ystradfellte. Here is a stretch of the road, in open countryside, which you can walk to this day. It's an eerie feeling walking such a road, knowing that hundreds of years ago Roman soldiers marched that way. At one spot there is a big stone, Moel Madoc, which stands in tribute to a Roman legionary who died in the area.

Saundersfoot is a neighbour of Tenby on the Pembrokeshire coast. Now, whereas half my family are from Tenby, I have always had a sneaking regard for Saundersfoot as well. This is because all our early holidays, when my son was very young, were spent in Saundersfoot. We never told him we were going on holiday until the morning of departure, and then he got very excited. I remember when I was young and was about to be taken to my grandparents in Tenby, the night before was always one of lack of sleep, because of the sheer anticipation of it all. We three, Elaine, Richard and myself, as a small branch of the Noble family, have had tremendous times in Saundersfoot. We always stayed in the Cambrian Hotel. This was prior to its collapse following an explosion in a neighbouring shop. The hours were spent on the beach, on the harbour wall and sometimes on boats that took us around Caldey Island. An odd incident happened here, too. I remember losing my car keys on the beach. They completely disappeared in the sand and were not to be seen anywhere. The

following day I returned to what I considered to be the same point on the beach and there they were, poking out of the sand, some 10 yards from me. I know it is only a small incident, but things like that tend to stick in the mind. On the radio programme in the morning, I have a phrase which says, "You can't legislate for it", and that was certainly so on that occasion. It reminded me of the story of a couple who were engaged just before World War II but because the man went away for six years, their relationship dwindled and ended. Both married someone else, but 30 or so years later, both their partners passed away. There came a day when the lady parked in a certain car park in a town in South Wales and her pre-war lover actually parked next to her. So you see, as with my keys, fate sometimes works in small ways, but as with that other occurrence, it also sometimes goes into overdrive and "you just can't legislate for it." You just have to accept it with an air of "what is meant to be is meant to be". (The Cambrian Hotel has been rebuilt and is looking as good as ever).

Senghenydd is famous in Wales for all the wrong reasons. Twice in its history there has been a massive mining disaster there, and on October 14th, 1913 a black record was broken when 439 men and boys were killed. Senghenydd for me, though, was a stop on my teaching trail and I was very happy there. It is almost a dead-end valley, but you can rise out of Senghenydd and take the mountain road over the top, which has fine views as you head towards Nelson. It is a road that closes very quickly on snowy days in winter. The school was on the side of the hill, but has now been replaced by a new building which is almost on the site of the old Universal Colliery, the one that blew up in 1913. If you visit the village today, you will note that there is a saw mill and a bus garage on the actual site. I remember playing rugby for Senghenydd R.F.C. whilst I was in college. They were very short at the time and they had sent down to the college for any spare bodies. I was very spare – I wasn't required by any of the college teams. It was in 1962 and here lies a confession, because, for travelling to Senghenydd, I received 7s. 6d. boot money. I played just twice and it was rumoured that they were prepared to offer me 10s. 6d. just to stay away. From my teaching days, though, I still have many friends in Senghenydd and I returned there recently on the occasion of the village carnival. It was a good day and I hope it continues for many years to come.

The Severn Bridge changed my life. In my early years in the profession, I was teaching in the Bath area. I was also courting at the time, and Friday night and Sunday night I travelled the great loop around the Severn Estuary, via Gloucester.

I was fortunate to be given a lift most weekends with a soldier who, oddly enough, was from Brynaman, my home village. He had a Mini Cooper S and radar eyes, for which I was grateful in that the journey was fast and safe, his keen sight being particularly useful when the mist was rolling off the Severn.

The Bridge, when it opened, was a revelation and I recall that on our very first journey over the brand-new short-cut to Wales there were shouts of Hallelujah all round. It was quite an exciting day, and we opened the car windows just to savour the experience further.

I have to say I love all bridges because they give you a real sense of going somewhere, but my first trip over the Severn was special – it meant an hour's extra courting, for a start.

SKIRRID MOUNTAIN INN, LLANFIHANGEL CRUCORNEY

Judge Jeffries slept here. Well at least Judge Jeffries hanged here. No, it wasn't a portrait, he was busily maintaining law and order in his own particular way. It is said that if you go to the well of the stairway in the inn, you can still see the mark of the rope that dispensed instant justice – or injustice – to those unfortunate enough to cross paths with Judge Jeffries. On a television programme concentrating on the borderlands of England and Wales, I was privileged to film at the inn, where many locals were recruited as extras. It has a friendly atmosphere and has an air about it which makes it important in the area. The landlady at the time was to be commended for her hospitality and good fare. It is said to be the oldest public house in Wales, and that fact alone merits an expedition to seek it out. Looking east from the inn, you see the Skirrid Mountain. What a magical place it seems, and its shape suggests that it must have been of some importance to the ancient peoples who inhabited the region.

The highest peak in Wales surely has to be included on any personal tour of Wales.

It is always impressive, whether brooding under low cloud in winter, standing clear on a fine day in summer or shimmering in its white mantle of snow as winter begins to wonder about giving way to spring.

I have been to the summit four times, but I've never climbed Snowdon. I know, I know, where is my spirit of adventure and the gung-ho determination that moves men to seek new horizons? I must have missed that course, for I confess to enjoying my comforts and that is illustrated by the fact that I travelled to Snowdon's summit by the famous train.

The view that impresses me most is that from the last station before the summit. The prospect as you look down into the Llanberis Pass is stupendous, and makes me feel that I should be roped to something solid, just in case.

I always find Llanberis, at the base of Snowdon, to be of great interest. I have stayed there on numerous occasions and there is a very interesting bistro there which will definitely be included if ever I write a book on great oases on the Welsh trailways.

St. David's was the venue for the very first school trip I organised – not as a teacher but as a pupil. I was chairman of the Arts Society in Amman Valley Grammar School in 1960 (only because I did art) and on a day of misplaced zeal, I attended the AGM. I learned early in life that if you attend an AGM, you tend to get elected for something.

The Bishop's Palace and St. David's Cathedral are fine historic and religious edifices in honour of our patron saint, and the village-sized city in the far, far West of Pembrokeshire is a right and proper place indeed for our patron saint because it takes a pilgrimage to get there, which gives a sense of achievement to those who live far away.

On a religious note, I was once told by a friend that he had trouble with three of the Ten Commandments, but he comforted himself in the knowledge that he felt a mark of seven out of ten is an 'A' grading in any exam. It is also interesting to recall that had there been an Eleventh Commandment saying "Though shalt not indulge in sharp practice", a certain Bishop of Saint David's would have had a real problem with it. Bishop William Barlow (1536-1548) stripped the lead roof off the Bishop's Palace and shipped it away to

provide a dowry for his five daughters.

Near St David's is Whitesand Bay, where many years ago I encountered the freshest sea in which I have ever dared to go beyond my bathing suit top. It was a beautiful sunny day I remember, and as I ventured forth into the briny the waves were coming in like rollers of foam delivered direct from America. Every tenth wave appeared to be a bit of a rogue,

charging up the beach with the power to rip off your bathing suit, or at least have it down to your knees, as was the case with one or two other people I noticed further along the foreshore.

The "power shower" was allowed to operate for only a short time before one of the local Greek gods, who were members of the 1960s version of *Baywatch,* ordered us all out of the sea.

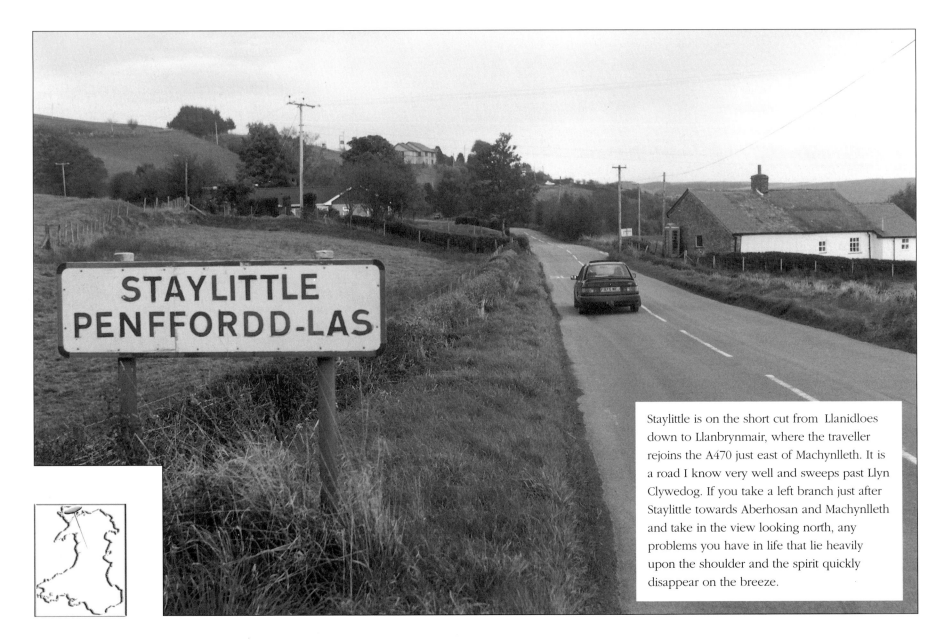

Staylittle is on the short cut from Llanidloes down to Llanbrynmair, where the traveller rejoins the A470 just east of Machynlleth. It is a road I know very well and sweeps past Llyn Clywedog. If you take a left branch just after Staylittle towards Aberhosan and Machynlleth and take in the view looking north, any problems you have in life that lie heavily upon the shoulder and the spirit quickly disappear on the breeze.

Storey Arms lies at the foot of Pen-y-Fan on the main Merthyr Tydfil to Brecon road. It's a very popular setting-off point for climbers and walkers. It's not a pub, but it was once. It lost its licence many years ago when the estate on which it stands was bought by a temperance man.

It also featured large on my radio programme for a while when we were seeking out the wettest and coldest places in Wales. The name Storey Arms always cropped up. It was sometime later that we realised that Storey Arms was one of the few places that had the instruments to measure precipitation and temperature and also bothered to send in the information. Another such place was St Harmon, in the mountains above Rhayader. Consequently, both names were at the top of the league for being amongst the wild places of Wales, weatherwise. Other places either didn't have the instruments or were keeping quiet about their situation.

As a child my visits to Swansea Bay were sporadic but pleasant. I remember the beach was fine, but the sea was always a far horizon away. The memories of the big iron bridge that took you across the busy Mumbles road, the floral clock below the bridge and the gardens there are still clear in my mind.

We would spend the day on the sand. We very rarely went into the sea because of the long walk – and about two hundred yards before you reached the water, you sank knee deep in a very fine, slimy mud.

No day was complete, however, without a ride to Mumbles on the Mumbles Railway. Oh, the tragedy of closing that railway down. In those days, there was also a railway line that ran along the embankment of Swansea Bay, taking people to the west. One of my most poignant memories is of leaving the old Victoria Station, Swansea, on one of those trains. As we passed Swansea Jail, one of the prisoners had his arm out of the window and he had a handkerchief in his hand, waving it as the train went by. It struck me, even as a young boy, as a very sad sight. I still wonder who he was.

This is a place long associated with broadcasting in Wales, and is famous for the first broadcast of Dylan Thomas's *Under Milk Wood*. There are many other points worthy of note about the building, but for me there is a strange connection. As a young boy, whenever our family had occasion to visit Swansea the South Wales Transport bus would stop at Trinity Place, by the bombed church. Trinity Place was just across the road from where the BBC building is now. Who would have thought that I would be working so close to that bus-stop so many years later?

One of the things my mother always insisted upon if we went to Swansea was a meal first, shopping afterwards. Even if we wanted a suit for a funeral or something, the meal took priority. The place to go, my mother decided, was the Windsor Cafe. Why? Well, the waitresses were all dressed in proper black-and-white uniforms and you didn't have a cup of tea, you had a pot of tea. I was always rather unhappy that you had to share tables, but that was the case in every cafe. I remember my uncle was with us on more than one occasion, and I was told that one of the waitresses quite fancied him, so we had good portions when he was with us. The other plus was that you had bread and butter with your fish and chips. This place of fine cuisine is still there and I visit it occasionally.

Sycharth is not well signposted but is near Llansilyn, not far from Oswestry. For years it was the home of Owain Glyndŵr, and you can stand on the modest site and wonder, in that beautiful setting, about the part it played in the dramatic military history of Wales.

Tairgwaith is a village out on a limb not far from Gwaun Cae Gurwen. It was set up to accommodate men who came down to work in the coalmines of the area. My father worked in those mines, too – first in Steer Pit and then in East Pit. I often travelled the road from Gwaun Cae Gurwen to Tairgwaith just to see where he worked. It was also the village nearest to the place where my grandfather was killed. My grandfather died in Steer Pit, and I well remember the day his best friend came home to tell us of the accident. It was not unusual for a miner in dirty clothes to walk the roads in those days because there were no pit-head baths, but to come home between shifts to a street in which he didn't live boded ill. I was ill in bed on the day that it happened. I was seven years of old. My mother was shaking the mat out of the upstairs window when she suddenly said that David John was coming. David John was a great pal of my grandfather in work and play, but he didn't live in Chapel Street as we did, so the sight of him coming towards us along the street on that day indicated to my mother straight away that there was bad news. When she opened the door to him, he said, "Lewis is dead" – and that was it. He was kinder when he went on to tell my grandmother.

Tenby was a magical place for me. We holidayed there when I was a boy because my grandparents on my father's side were from Tenby, and lived their latter years there at No. 8 Trafalgar Road, next-door to the barber's shop.

My grandfather was a painter, not on canvas, but a painter of houses – although there were a few artists in the family.

I still remember the front door. It had been grained in the manner that was fashionable then, where you combed through the paint. It was there for many years. To my regret I never bought the door; I always wanted to.

Tenby was an adventure playground for me because my grandfather had two small sailing yachts in the harbour. One was called the *Doric* and the other the *Elsie*. Of course, when I went back home to Brynaman after the holiday I added several feet to their length when discussing my adventures with friends.

As well as taking part in many yacht races in Tenby, we were allowed to go out mackerel fishing in the *Doric*, and it was exciting going out on excursions as far as Caldey Island.

For me Castle Hill was also an adventure playground. Just off-shore of Castle Hill is Saint Catherine's Island, where the former fort can still be seen. For a while I went through a phase of thinking that the place would be a marvellous place to live, but then again with the tidal flow you'd only get visitors twice a day.

My grandfather also had a shed on the top floor of an old building behind the present Tenby Yacht Club, and I can still recall the smell of the creosote, paint, ropes and nets that he kept there.

I remember, too, the Royal Gate House Hotel, looking down on the North Beach. As I passed the hotel, I could see people in the restaurant, and I often wondered who could afford to go in to a restaurant like that. They must have been rich. One day, I thought, one day maybe I'll be able to do that.

I have the honour of being Tenby Male Choir's president. Although I have very convivial relationships with many of the Welsh male voice choirs, my attachment to Tenby is special in view of my family connection with the town.

Elaine and I have enjoyed many cordial and happy occasions in their company. One incident stays in the mind, however, and it involved a "nearly" concert tour to Romania. The choir actually did go to Romania, but Elaine and I did not. Our withdrawal was last-minute – so last-minute that the aircraft's propellers had started to turn.

Elaine during that period was a fearful flyer and when she saw a tired, Russian-built Ilyushin 18 arrive from Romania at Cardiff Airport to collect the Tenby Choir, her existing misgivings were magnified.

This period was the pre-revolution era in Romania and the regime was strict. The security officer on the aircraft was a big woman, dressed in a leather trenchcoat of early-007 vintage. She insisted on seeing all passports herself and all suitcases had to be lined up on the airport tarmac. She insisted that "the Presidente" sit in the VIP section, which turned out to be a claustrophobic arrangement of seats near the tail of the plane.

Elaine's nervousness went into turbo mode and she insisted we leave the aircraft. The situation had not been helped by a series of telephone calls I had received from someone working in broadcasting in London. The calls, in a heavy mid-European accent, went along the lines of "I hear you are going with a choir to Bucharest – I would like you to take into the country some medicine for my family. If you do this, someone will contact you at your hotel room".

I'd had visions of me becoming a Foreign Office statistic and I had declined the courier offer.

So we got off the aircraft, leaving the Tenby Choir to tour without us. My last image, however, is of myself, the pilot and the large, leather-clad security woman searching the bowels of the aircraft's luggage bay.

She had insisted that if we were getting off the plane, then our cases must get off the plane, too. I didn't argue.

The Black Mountain is on the western edge of the Brecon Beacons, and it's a kind of spiritual home for me because it stands to the north of Brynaman, my home village. It was a great playground area. The rivers that flowed down from it had deep pools for summer bathing and the great moorland spaces were areas for cowboys and indians to have a go at each other. There was also a place called Tro Derlwyn, the Derlwyn Turn, where an unofficial rubbish dump had accumulated over the years. It was at the bottom of a fairly deep ravine. There were interesting items down there, like the remains of old lorries that hadn't quite made it around the corner. A story arose among the boys that a skeleton had been found there of a person with a very, very long nose, who had been a mystery passenger on one of these lorries. Actually, on checking the story out some years later, I found that only one lorry had gone over the edge, and the driver had jumped out safely. So what of the skeleton at the bottom of the ravine? Well, the long-nosed human turned out to be a sheep.

On one of our expeditions across the mountain, in this case to Carreg Cennen Castle, I was with John Salter, who is now an engine driver on the railways, and Tecwin "Tiger Tim" Thomas. On the return journey we were late leaving Carreg Cennen. Consequently, the mist and the darkness came down upon us as we came up over the Black Mountain to get back towards Brynaman. By this time my mother had called the police because we were officially lost. There weren't many cars in those days, and the only two which passed us on the mountain road were unable to give us a lift because they were full. On reaching the top of the Black Mountain, before we started the descent towards Brynaman, we saw another car take shape out of the murk.

Sure enough, it held a courting couple. It must have caused them a huge amount of stress and fear to have three fellows coming out of the darkness and banging on the car while they were in the middle of their courting. Thankfully, they did give us a lift back to the village. They married later in life – I suppose having had that experience they felt they had to.

DAVID DAVIES AGE 22 YEARS
OF GLYNCLAWDD FARM GWYNFE
WAS KILLED AT THIS SPOT ON
THE 21ST MAY 1884 HIS HORSE
BOLTED AND HE FELL UNDER THE
WHEEL OF HIS CART WHICH WAS
LADEN WITH LIME

As you climb out of Treorchy in the Rhondda Fawr on the road that leads to Nant-y-moel and Ogmore Vale, there is a lay-by near the summit, just at the junction that branches away to drop towards Cymer and Port Talbot.

On many days there is an ice-cream van in that lay-by. It was certainly there on the day when I drove from Ogmore Vale to Aberdare, via the Bwlch and Treorchy. It was a day in March and the strengthening spring sunshine gave way to cloud and then a heavy snow shower as I approached the summit.

As I passed the lay-by, there it was, the ice-cream van, surrounded by the locals – a few valley sheep. I drove on, and I was suddenly struck by the thought that I'd never eaten ice-cream in the snow before, so I stopped, turned the car around and returned to the tableau I'd just witnessed. The lady in charge of the van was, as expected I suppose, of Italian blood. She did not drive and her husband, having delivered her there in the morning, was due to collect her at tea-time. We chatted for some time: I licked my ice-cream cone and chocolate flake and she periodically fed the sheep with the odd wafer. It was a surreal scene there in the snow shower – but you've got to do these things now and again, don't you think?

Llawhaden Castle

I include it because I'd like to stand on it. The line is in many ways mythical, but yet it marks a definite line separating the north of Pembrokeshire from the southern part of the county.

My family on my father's side were very much from "down below", with that marked accent that is very much South Pembrokeshire, as opposed to the more Welsh-language-based north.

I know that the Landsker Line passes on a rough bearing from east to west and passes through Haverfordwest, but where is the track exactly, so that I may stand on it, one leg in the north, the other "down below"?

These were the buses that visited Brynaman twice a week, on Tuesdays and Fridays. They came from "over the top" – the Black Mountain – bringing people to visit the Brynaman Public Hall cinema. Our family used them as well, to visit relatives on "the other side" who lived on a farm near Gwynfe. The Black Mountain for me was a "great divide" separating industrial South Wales from the rural expanses to the north. The Thomas Bros coaches were, therefore, a symbol of a journey into a different world. For the return journey the passengers from "over the top" were picked up at the local fish-and-chip shop, the bus driver having parked for a restful few hours near Gibea Chapel cemetery for a bit of private courting.

What an inspirational place Tower Colliery has become since it was bought by its own miners. It is a fitting place of pilgrimage to honour the men who dug in and said, "No! Enough is enough! Officialdom is wrong – we can make this place work." And didn't they just.

Tower Colliery is now a symbol of triumphant enterprise by a workforce who were determined to save their jobs, and it is understandable that there are worldwide approaches from people who just want to visit and stand on what they consider to be almost hallowed ground.

On a journey from south to north, having first got around the corners of the tortuous but scenic route through Mid Wales, beyond Dolgellau you come across a long straight road heading north, parallel to the old Roman road Sarn Helen. At the end of the long stretch of the A470 is the village of Trawsfynydd. Alongside it is a lake and beyond it is a scene that reminds me of the old *Quatermass* series on television – the Trawsfynydd Nuclear Power Station. Trawsfynydd is not a village you would call into if you were on a journey from south to north – or going in the opposite direction. But I have on occasion, from sheer interest, called in. It is a village where all the houses are built of the local stone, so it is a true village of North Wales. It was given added prominence when a film was made about Hedd Wyn, the renowned poet of the area, who was killed in World War I. I have found the village, which is bypassed so easily, intriguing, with its own drawing power. I have made a promise to myself that one of these days I am going to stay the night in Trawsfynydd. I know of a tale of miners who went to Trawsfynydd during the strike of the 1980s. They were allocated picketing duties at the Trawsfynydd

Power Station. I do believe that several became friendly with the local villagers and relationships between picketers, villagers and even the local police became the stuff that television drama of the *'Allo, 'Allo* kind is made.

This is a fine house and well worth a visit if you are in the area. The fact that it has associations with Captain Henry Morgan, the pirate, gives it very good credentials. In the company of John Dee, the astrologer on my morning radio programme, I once spent some hours on the top floor of Tredegar House. It's said that there is a resident ghost. People who work there would have you believe that of an evening when they lock up, they close most of the doors, and when they arrive again the following morning, some of the doors are open. I don't know whether this is true, but all I can say is that after a few hours on the top floor with John Dee, both of us felt decidedly uncomfortable. The hairs on the backs of our necks were not exactly standing on end, but there was sufficient electricity in the air to make us agree that we would not wish to spend the night there.

Trefil is a small village just to the north of the Yellow Brick Road – the A465 Heads of the Valleys route to the stars. I have spoken at the rugby club dinner there twice, and on each occasion it was a convivial and welcoming experience. Who was that fellow who started his soup before grace? Trefil, like Deri and Bedlinog, is a marvellous place to enjoy rugby and village hospitality.

Trefil RFC have a wonderful means of conveyance – the Black and Red Devil. It is an ex-Blaenau Gwent day ambulance with the hydraulic hoist for wheelchairs still attached to the rear of the vehicle. It has 20-something seats, so it is really a bus, and is used regularly on weekends for team transport and for ferrying those over the limit back to their homes once "Time" is called. For those unable to climb the steps of the bus on such occasions, then the hydraulic lift must be a tremendous boost.

Beyond Trefil, if you take the mountain road, you come to a dead end. The road leads to a quarry, the scene, so I'm told, of clandestine courtships and unofficial liaisons. This was in the past, of course, and I wouldn't know too much about such things, anyway.

What is beyond doubt is the magnificent vista that unfolds as you drive towards the quarry. The view to the north, looking towards the Usk Valley and Mid Wales, is wonderful. The road along the route is not in good repair and care should be taken, but the scene awaits even if you cycle or walk the road's length.

The valley that runs up from Lampeter towards Tregaron and on to Pontrhydfendigaid is supremely beautiful. I had forgotten how attractive it was until I returned there recently to view the trotting races. I have been invited to speak at Tregaron Rugby Football Club on three occasions, but unfortunately I haven't been able to make it because of prior commitments. Possibly fate is being kind to me, because I have heard that such occasions are really a three-day event.

The valley stretches northwards towards Pontrhydfendigaid past the Tregaron Bog, which is a unique area of great interest to naturalists and botanists.

When I was in the sixth form in Amman Valley Grammar School we were taken to the area by the geography master to study the bog itself, and also to visit a farm on which lived unique brothers. Apparently, the men were prime examples of a lineage that had come down from the Bronze Age. No one in their family had ever owned a bike, so there had been no intermingling of the blood. It was a delicate visit in that we were told by the geography master to view the men keenly and take sneak looks at their foreheads and noses, without the men themselves realising we were doing so. "Take a sneak look, but don't stare" was the order of the day. I'm sure the brothers realised why we were there, and even now I'm not sure whether the visit to the farm was official or otherwise.

WELSH SHEEP!

Now there are many varieties and breeds of sheep in Wales, but the ones that are common to my area are the Welsh Glamorgan sheep. If sheep were divided into regiments, then the Welsh Glamorgan would be the SAS. They are not as often seen in the streets of the valleys now as they used to be, but when bin days and refuse collection days in our area were regularly on Mondays and Thursdays, the sheep seemed to know this. Late at night the ewes and rams would roam the streets and come around butting the lids off the

dustbins. There was a two-fold motive for this. One, their efforts provided them with food. Two, they were training their lambs to do the same when they matured.

Some of the sheep in the area were regulars, and you got to know their bleats. One of them seemed to have a bronchial cough with its bleat and you felt a little concern for its health. On other occasions you would hear a ewe bleating constantly because she had lost her lamb. Half an hour later the lamb would be

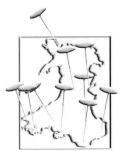

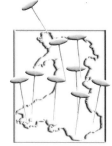

coming around your street bleating constantly because she had lost her mother. Such is the guile and cleverness of these local sheep that I remember a marvellous comment by Dai Jones of Llanilar. Amongst his many attributes and talents, he is, after all, a farmer, so one should listen to his country wisdom. The only way to keep a Welsh sheep safe in its place, he said, is to have it in your freezer, but with those Glamorgan sheep, you have to lock the freezer as well.

The valley that leads from Newtown to Welshpool is near sea level. The hills that line the valley are the kind that children will draw in painting lessons – neat, rounded and definite. Children always draw good hills, but not such good trees. Infants will draw "lollipop" trees and there are few of these in the countryside; but as for hills, they've got them well sorted out. Have a look at the hills on either side of this road – aren't they impressive?

Ystradfellte is renowned for its river and waterfall scenery and is an area of quite magnificent walks and picturesque views. Pontneddfechan has a charm of its own at the head of the Neath Valley, and there are fine vistas as you look down the Valley itself.

I was headteacher of Ysgol Thomas Stephens for seven years, and enjoyed my time there immensely. The school lies opposite the Glynneath Golf Club, whose president is one Max Boyce. My executive duties as a headteacher would, on occasion, see me shooting past the golf club chasing the dinner van up to Ystradfellte School. Our school canteen provided Ystradfellte School with all meals. Very often the custard or the gravy was left behind and I had to take it up in the boot of my car. There were very few occasions when I caught the van, and the custard generally arrived a little later than the pudding, and the gravy, on occasion, didn't make it to the dinner at all. That was clearly my fault, but it was always a lovely journey to travel, even if the gravy had a crust on it by the time I got to Ystradfellte.

On one occasion, I thought it a good idea to hold a pets morning in school. Most children brought their usual domestic pets, but one child turned up with a rabbit and another with a ferret. There were one or two consequences, I have to say. I return to Pontneddfechan quite often these days because there are interesting hostelries to visit and support.

ℐNDEX